How to Face the Health Challenges while Growing Old.

What happens to your Heart, Brain, Kidneys, Lungs, Ear, Nose, Throat, Bones & Joints as you age. Get to know Diabetes, Thyroid, Nutritional and Medical Problems of the elderly.

Problems of the Elderly Book 1

Sahasranam Kalpathy

COPYRIGHT

ISBN: 9798359264969
Imprint: Independently published

Disclaimer

All the facts in the books and the statistics given are taken from authentic sources. The diagrams in the book are the author's own and drawn by the author himself and not reproduced from any other source. However, the personal opinions expressed throughout the book are the author's own.

I dedicate this book to my good friend

Prof. R. Krishnan

Senior Consultant in General Medicine

A true friend, philosopher, and guide

who has stood by me through thick and thin

Table of Contents

PREFACE

What provoked me to write this book

My interest in aging started when I turned seventy. Mentally, I thought that I was young, but my physique refused to follow my mind. Minor medical problems cropped up and I began complaining a lot. My wife used to tell me "Hi, dear, you are getting old. Reconcile to that. Your mental age and your chronological age are at loggerheads. Accept the fact and learn to live with it."

Yes, this was a genuine fact of life. *We, as the elderly know what it is to be young and energetic, but the youngsters of today do not know what it is to be old and frail.* They assume that their parents and other elders are still as full of stamina and strength as they had a couple of decades ago. They do not understand the vagaries of old age. This unfortunate fact is another reason for the genesis of this book.

Yes, true. I could see that I was growing old. But the subtle changes seen in me slowly creeping up gnawing at my body and disheartening my spirit told me that I better take heed of nature's warning. This got me thinking. What are the *'normal'* changes that occur with age and when should we consider it abnormal enough to seek the help of a physician.

This was the central idea around which this book developed. I decide to work on this and gathered information on the changes that occur in a normal person with age and what an individual could do to recognize them and take preventing measures to postpone the inevitable.

I have not ventured in this book to discuss in detail the diseases of the elderly and their treatment. I would like to emphasize the fact that _this book is not a substitute for the physician_. It is a book for the common man. It is only a handbook for the elderly. The book highlights the changes that occur in our body as we age and prepare us to face them. I have also endeavored to explain in detail the preventive measures that we can adopt to postpone these degenerative changes of aging. Rather, I felt that an awareness of what aging could do to your body and mind was in order. And this book is the result of such a quest on my part.

It was when these thoughts were assailing my mind that Prof. R Krishnan of the department of Medicine in the Baby Memorial Hospital where I was the Senior consultant and Chief of medical services, decided to organize a Seminar on the 'Problems of the Elderly'. He summoned an impressive assemblage of specialists to speak on the various aspects of aging and their diseases. The seminar was a tremendous success. Professor Krishnan was a vibrant character and his enthusiasm was contagious. He reminded me of an experiment my teacher demonstrated when I was a high school student. The teacher demonstrated what happens when a blob of sodium is dropped into a jar of water. Imagine the turbulence and the explosive result that followed. Well, Professor Krishnan reminded me of that blob of sodium.

This set me thinking. Why should I not make this knowledge available to a wider global non-medical audience. The inevitability of aging and death is something every one accepts. As the saying goes, *'Everyone wants to go to heaven, but no one wants to die'.* Likewise, everyone wants to live long, but no one wants to grow old.

I began gathering information on all aspects of normal aging from various sources and decided to share it with my readers by publishing it as a book.

As far as possible, I have avoided the use of medical terms in the book. And, wherever medical terms had to be used, for the benefit of the reader, I have included a **Glossary** at the end of the book where these terms have been explained. Also, the font of the paperback version of the book is kept larger so as to enable the senior citizens to read the book with ease.. A brief description of the anatomy of each organ system is also provided at the beginning of each chapter. This is optional for the reader and may be skipped without affecting the understanding of the rest of the book. An occasional scientifically inclined reader, however, may find this section useful. The anatomical diagrams are simple sketches drawn by me to give the reader a basic understanding of the human anatomy. Only a few of the common diseases are discussed under each organ system.

As the volume of information grew, I decided to publish the book as a series and I humbly present to you the Part 1 of this series.

Dr. K. V. Sahasranam

(Sahasranam Kalpathy)

INTRODUCTION

Everybody wants to live long, but nobody wants to grow old. Aging is a natural process, which presents a unique challenge for all sections of the society. It is surmised that the number of people in the world above age 60 will increase to 1.2 billion in 2025 and subsequently to two billion in 2050 according to the World Health Organization (WHO). To add to the burden, about 75% of these elderly individuals will be living in the developing nations utilizing the economy of those countries and the overburdened health care delivery systems there.

Furthermore, chronic diseases, physical disabilities, mental illnesses, and other co-morbidities plague the elderly and make their life miserable. Other problems that haunt them are physical and financial constraints, food and nutritional issues, isolation from society, emotional and psychological concerns like children abandoning them or maltreating them. These factors render aging as a challenge to individuals.

Globally, the life expectancy of an average person was 45.51 years in 1950 which has risen to 72.98 years in 2022.

The life expectancy in India in 1950 was 35.21 years, 1970 was 49.7 years and has risen to 70.19 years in 2022. Life expectancy in the US in 1950 was 68.14 years and increased to 79.05 years in 2022. It fell from 78.9 years in 2019 to 76.6 years in 2021. This decline is mainly due to the Covid-19 pandemic. The life expectancy in the United Kingdom in 1950 was 68.69 years and it rose to 81.65 years in 2022.

Sir Christopher Booth, who discovered the absorption of Vitamin B12 *"wrote with sadness but with detachment about his transition from youth to old age, from a healthy carefree existence to dependence to hospital: he reminds us how, as one gets older, disability strikes suddenly, severely, ferociously, furiously, with the person and his family often totally unprepared"*.

Life expectancy is the key metric used for assessing the health of the population. However, there is a difference in the health administration in different nations. But in the modern world as the health improves owing to the developments in modern medicine, the death rate has come down and the life expectancy has gone up. Since 1900 the global life expectancy has almost doubled and now stands above 70 years in most countries of the world.

The death rate (*Deaths per 1000 people*) has also declined over the years. In 1950, the Global death rate was 20.15 whereas it has significantly declined to 7.678 in 2022.

The death rate in India was 28.161 in 1950 which declined to 7.38 in 2022. The death rate in the United States was 9.649 in 1950 and declined to 8.782 in 2019. But it has been 9.075 in 2022 owing to the recent Covid-19 pandemic.

This decline in death rate and the increasing longevity in countries is leading to an increase in the population of the elderly more than 65 years of age globally.

This poses problems to the society and to the relatives of the elderly. Also, it causes a heavy burden on the health services in the country, especially when it is subsidized by the government.

Geriatrics, (*geron= old man, and iatros = healing [Greek]*) , *is a sub-specialty of medicine which deals with diseases of older individuals and health care of the Elderly.* The word denotes the branch of medicine or social science dealing with the health and care of old people, whereas **Gerontology** is a study of the aging process itself. It is the study of the social, psychological & biological aspects of aging, the study of the aging process itself, and its science. Gerontologists are researchers and practitioners in various fields of biology, medicine, pharmacy, nursing, public health, optometry, dentistry, social work, physical & occupational therapy, psychology, psychiatry, sociology, economics, political science, architecture, housing & anthropology -all related to different aspects of aging.

The term **Geriatrics** first coined in 1909 by Ignatz Leo Nascher, Austrian-American doctor, then Chief of Mount Sinai Hospital, New York, translates into 'care of aged people'. A **Geriatrician** is a physician who specializes in the care of elderly people.

WHO has defined *'elderly'* as individuals with a chronological age of 65 years and above.

Prof. Bernard Isaacs of the University of Birmingham, popularized this specialty owing to his enthusiasm and passion He is credited with listing the four 'Giant' problems of Geriatrics namely - *Immobility, Instability, Incontinence* and *Intellectual impairment*; he also identified the common causes for admission to a Geriatric unit: expectation of therapeutic recovery, medical urgency (the need for hospital care), and basic care (being unfit to fend for themselves in providing food, warmth, and cleanliness).

The medical problems of the elderly are different from those of younger or middle-aged individuals. Many biological, molecular, and structural changes occur with aging. Unlike in the young, the physiological reserve in the elderly is reduced and hence they are unable to cope up with even minor physiological insults or variations like dehydration, mild diarrhea , a mild fever, or changes in the environmental temperature. For the elderly, the quality of life is more important than the quantity of life ahead of them.

Diseases in the elderly may present atypically, for example a fever may present as a delirium which may be misinterpreted as a psychological abnormality. The fever is liable to be missed.

Sometimes, what looks like a mere giddiness or confusion, may be indicative of a severe heart attack. The symptoms may be totally unnatural and the diagnosis is liable to be missed.

Impaired vision and hearing are the two most important and inevitable problems of the elderly.

Elderly individuals would like to live independently as long as possible without resorting to outside help. In this context the activities of daily living and self-help pose the greatest challenges to them.

Frailty also poses a big obstacle in old age especially in women. *Unintentional weight loss, muscle weakness, exhaustion, low physical activity, and slowed walking speed* have been described as the five main attributes of frailty.

Often the biological age and the chronological age of an individual do not run parallel. An 80-year-old may have the physical and mental capacity of a 50-year-old and vice versa. Such a diversity is not uncommon with aging. Socrates is said to have learnt to play musical instruments when he was eighty. Michael Angelo was painting his great masterpieces when he was eighty. Isaac Newton was working hard even when he was eighty five. Former US president Herbert Hoover was active even at eighty eight. Goethe was said to have finished Faust when he was ninety-two. These examples bear ample proof to the fact that anyone can be active even when old. Our body retires when we cross sixty, but our mind never retires and we should not let it to. We need to have an open mind like an umbrella, most useful when it is open.

In this book, which is the first part of the series, the problems related to the Heart, Lungs, Kidneys, Brain, Endocrine glands, Ear, Nose, Throat, Bones & Joints, and Nutrition in the elderly are discussed. The next book will deal with more systems.

Resources

1. Krishnan, R. Introduction to the Monograph. BMH Medical Journal - ISSN 2348–392X, [S.l.], v. 7, n. Suppl, p. S2-S7, Feb. 2020. ISSN 2348-392X.)

2. United Nations – World Population Prospects 2022

3. Christopher Booth in Oxford Textbook of Medicine (5 ed.-2010) Eds. David A. Warrell, Timothy M. Cox, and John D. Firth

4. By the 2022 American Geriatrics Society Beers Criteria® Update Expert Panel. American

Chapter 1. HEART – CIRULATORY SYSTEM

Structure & Function. The **Circulatory System** *functions to distribute blood to the different parts of the body. The heart is the main organ of the circulatory system. It is an incredible muscular organ that works incessantly during the whole lifetime of a person. The normal heart is the size of one's closed fist and, pumps blood throughout the body through a network of blood vessels. The heart weighs around 9-12 ounces (250-350 grams). It is situated in the chest cage slightly to the left, protected by the breastbone in front and the spine at the back. It has four chambers. The two upper chambers on the right and left are called the **Atria**. (singular: Atrium) and the lower chambers on the right and left are called **Ventricles**. The Atria receive the blood from all over the body and the ventricles pump out the blood.*

*Two large blood vessels bring blood to the heart and join the Right Atrium (**RA**). They are called **Veins**. One large vein called the **Superior Vena Cava (SVC)** brings blood from the upper part of the body and another, the **Inferior Vena Cava (IVC)** brings blood from the lower half of the body. On the left side, four veins named **Pulmonary veins (PV)** bring blood to the left atrium (**LA**) from the lungs. (**See Fig.1**)*

*One large blood vessel called the **Aorta** arises from the left ventricle (**LV**) and carries blood* to the various parts of the body through its branches. Similarly, one large blood vessel called the **Pulmonary Artery** carries blood from the right ventricle (**RV**) into the lungs. (See Diagram 1)

Arteries are the name given to blood vessels that carry blood away from the heart to various parts of the body. *Veins* are blood vessels that gather blood from various parts of the body and bring it to the heart. The Aorta is the largest artery in the body. It carries oxygen-rich blood to various parts of the body. The veins carry oxygen-poor-carbon dioxide-rich blood back to the heart. This is then pumped by the right ventricle into the lungs where the oxygen that we breathe in diffuses into the blood and the carbon dioxide diffuses out into the lungs to be breathed out.

When they reach the lungs or the different areas of the body, the arteries branch into smaller and smaller vessels, ultimately ending in thin hair like vessels called **Capillaries** which have a very thin walls through which substances from blood can diffuse into the tissues. The oxygen and other nutrients from the blood pass out of the capillaries into the tissues of the body and in turn carbon dioxide and other waste products of metabolism enter the capillaries. The capillaries join together to form larger and larger veins which ultimately enter the superior and inferior vena cava which carry this carbon dioxide-rich blood back to the heart to be sent to the lung for 'purification'. This completes the **Circulatory cycle**.

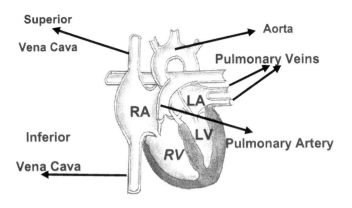

Figure 1 (Heart – Structure)

*Inside the heart the blood is allowed to flow only in one direction – " a sort of one-way-traffic" for the blood. The blood flows from the atria to the ventricles. It is prevented from flowing back to the atria by valves located between the atria and ventricles. On the right side it is called the Tricuspid valve (**TV**) and on the left side it is called the Mitral Valve (**MV**). Similarly, valves prevent the blood pumped from the ventricles to the aorta (**Aortic Valve- AV**) and pulmonary artery (**Pulmonary Valve-PV**) from leaking back into the ventricles. Thus, these four valves in the heart ensure that blood always flows 'forward' and never 'backward'.*

*The normal heart beats about 70 times a minute (60-100 beats per minute). This is possible because there is a tiny button-cell battery like structure located in the upper part of the right atrium called **Sinus Node**. This is the 'pulse generator' of the heart and gives small electrical signals or impulses regularly to the heart which trigger the heart to contract. These impulses are carried throughout the heart by a series of fiber like connections similar to the electrical wiring in our homes. The whole heart thus contracts simultaneously as one unit.*

The heart beats continuously during the life time of the individual. Between two contractions of the heart, it takes a few milliseconds of 'rest'. That is all the rest the heart gets. The heart beats about 1,00,000 times a day. Just imagine how many times it would beat during the lifetime of a person!

The heart helps to supply oxygen and nutrients carried in the blood to the various parts of the body. In turn the blood gathers carbon dioxide and other waste products from the various parts of the body. The carbon dioxide is blown out through the lungs when we breathe out and the other waste products are filtered out as urine by the kidneys. The pumping of the heart also helps to maintain the blood pressure of the individual.

*Even though the heart pumps 4 – 8 liters (1- 2 gallons) of blood per minute to all parts of the body, the heart needs to be supplied by blood separately to nourish itself. This is done through three small arteries called the **Coronary Arteries**. It is the blockage in these arteries that cause heart attacks in individuals.*

Like any organ of the body, the heart also undergoes changes with age. The heart which is a pump working day in and day out from one's birth until death hardly takes rest. The wear and tear that usually occurs in a mechanical pump does not usually affect the heart. However, age catches up with this wonderful pump and subjects it to various diseases as the person grows old.

The young resting heart beats at a regular rate of around 60-80 times per minute. But as the person ages, the cells which control the heart rate are reduced in number and consequently, the heart rate tends to become slower. The heart may increase in size slightly and become stiffer than it was in the young. The valves in the heart also tend to thicken and occasionally deposits of calcium are formed on these valves leading to decrease in their normal function. The blood vessels in the body thicken. Some medium sized arteries like those supplying the brain, the limbs, the abdominal organs, and the heart may tend to develop fatty deposits in their walls causing stiffening and narrowing of these arteries. The is called **Atherosclerosis** and is a major cause of heart disease leading to heart attacks and strokes. Decrease in blood supply to other organs, limbs or brain may also consequently occur. Occasionally the walls of the blood vessels may tend to weaken and cause a bulge or ballooning of the vessel. This leads to a condition called '**Aneurysm**'.

Approximately, 77.5% males and 74.5% females in the age group 65 – 79 have cardiovascular disease (diseases of the heart and blood vessels). This increases to 89.4% of males; 90.8% of females in those above 80. About 67.5% of males; 75.7% of females in the 65 – 75-year age group have high blood pressure whereas 7.5% of males; 3.9% of females have heart failure.

The main heart diseases that occur with increasing age are Coronary artery disease, Heart failure, High blood pressure, and Atrial fibrillation.

CORONARY ARTERY DISEASE

Narrowing of the blood vessels supplying the heart due to atherosclerosis is the most common heart disease leading to *morbidity* and *mortality* in the elderly. This is generally referred to as Coronary Artery Disease (**CAD**). A gradual narrowing of the three main blood vessels of the heart occurs leading to a decrease in blood supply to the heart. Occasionally there can be an abrupt block of the blood vessel causing a sudden cutting off the blood supply to the muscles of the heart leading to a heart attack.

The symptoms experienced by the patient during a heart attack are usually severe chest pain occurring in the centre of the chest. This pain may occasionally be felt in the shoulders or arms, lower jaw, neck or back. The pain is often intense and associated with profuse sweating.

However, in the aged population these typical symptoms described above may be absent and the patient may have only symptoms like breathlessness, severe tiredness, dizziness, loss of consciousness, or vomiting. Occasionally, sudden unexpected death may be the first symptom of a heart attack. Often these symptoms may mislead the relatives or caregiver to consider other illnesses and miss a heart attack. Hence one must be aware of this atypical presentation of symptoms in heart attacks in the aged individuals.

Prompt medical attention and hospitalisation is needed in these circumstances as a heart attack is an emergency that may be fatal.

When the narrowing of the coronary arteries are gradual over a prolonged period, the patient tends to feel symptoms only when he exerts himself. The classical symptom is pain occurring in the center of the chest on exertion relieved promptly with rest. When a person exerts, the heart rate increases, and this leads to an increase in the oxygen needed by the heart. Consequently, the heart, thus deprived of oxygen feels the pain. Just as in a heart attack, the pain may be felt in the center of the chest, shoulders, arms, neck, lower jaw or back. But the crucial point is that the pain is relieved as soon as the patient stops his exertion and takes rest. This condition is called "*Angina Pectoris.*" In the elderly, however, this may present atypically as breathlessness alone or severe fatigue on exertion with inability to move forward without any chest pain. Hence the real nature of the illness could be missed.

Angina pectoris also needs to be treated timely with measures to remove the block in the coronary arteries. Interventional procedures like coronary angioplasty which is quite common in the present times or coronary bypass surgery may be needed. Medications also relieve the pain in many patients and are always prescribed by the physician.

Following the heart attack or the treatment of angina, the patient must be on long term medications. The caregiver or relative should be careful to see that the patient takes his medications regularly.

Proper rehabilitation of the patient after a heart attack or treatment of angina pectoris will be advised by the cardiologist and this must be strictly followed to bring the patient back to his routine normal life.

What are the risk factors for developing CAD

There are many risk factors which lead to the development of CAD in individuals. These are common for the young, middle aged and the old. They can be divided into Non-modifiable risk factors which cannot be changed and Modifiable risk factors which can be changed by lifestyle modification or medical treatment. They are as follows.

Non-Modifiable Risk Factors

- **Age**. As the person becomes older, the risk of developing CAD increases. About 80% of deaths due to heart attacks occur in those above 80 years of age.
- **Sex**. Females below the age of fifty have a lesser risk of developing CAD compared to men. However, this risk decreases as they grow older or if they have surgical removal of their ovaries for medical reasons.
- **Family History of CAD**. Persons with a family history of premature CAD, i.e., the disease occurring before the age of fifty in men and sixty-five in women, have a higher chance of having the disease. The disease is 2 – 3-fold in them.

Modifiable Risk Factors

- **Smoking**. Smoking is a very strong risk factor for atherosclerosis, heart attacks and sudden death in a person.
- **Lack of physical activity**. Persons with sedentary habits, especially if they have other risk factors are more prone to CAD.
- **Increased blood cholesterol**.
     Increased levels of blood cholesterol is an important and common risk factor. The fraction of cholesterol in blood called the LDL cholesterol is the important culprit in causing atherosclerosis and CAD. Triglycerides is another component of blood fats which also is equally damaging to the arteries.
- **Overweight and Obesity**. These are also risk factors in the development of CAD.
- **Diabetes mellitus**. The risk of CAD is two to three times more in patients who are diabetic.
- **High Blood Pressure**. High blood pressure is a strong risk factor in the causation of CAD.
- **Psychosocial Stress**. Chronic stress, anxiety, and social isolation are also factors which can cause CAD.

Coronary Artery Disease (CAD) in Women

There is a widely held misconception that women are 'protected' against cardiovascular diseases. This is a wrong notion. The death due to CAD is 55% for women compared to 43% for men. In many of the countries of the world, CAD in women is under-detected and underdiagnosed. It is true that till the age of 50, CAD is more in men, but after the age of 60 it is equal in both sexes. By the seventh or eighth decade, CAD is more in women. One out of three deaths in women is due to CAD. Normally, women present with CAD approximately ten years later than men, mostly after the menopause. However, the risk factors like high blood pressure, diabetes, high cholesterol, and obesity increase the chances of developing CAD in women earlier in life.

In younger women, estrogens (female sex hormones) have a protective effect on heart disease, but this protection is lost after menopause. Women in whom the ovaries and uterus have been surgically removed for medical reasons have the same risk as men of developing CAD. Other risk factors are the same for men and women.

The symptoms of a heart attack may be atypical in women, especially in old age. In one study it was noted that 65% of women did not have the typical chest pain of myocardial infarction. Similarly, the death rate due to heart attacks is higher in women compared to men. Women are also at a higher risk of complications after a heart attack. It has also been observed that mortality after cardiac bypass surgery is more in women compared to men.

Hence any symptoms of heart disease in women, especially in old age should not be taken lightly and dismissed as trivial, since they could cause more serious complications, even death.

Prevention of Coronary Artery Disease

What can one do to prevent heart disease in old age? Truly speaking, the prevention of heart disease in old age should begin when one is young. The following are the main approaches which a person should follow to ward of heart disease and high blood pressure.

- **Exercise**. Being physically active with adequate exercise is one of the most important aspects of preventing heart disease and high blood pressure. At least 150 minutes of aerobic exercise per week is needed for cardiovascular fitness. Exercise should be done at least five days a week for 30-45 minutes daily. Simple exercises like walking briskly as the age and physical condition permits, dancing, gardening, cycling, swimming, jogging, playing badminton, or other simple non-contact sports are all helpful in maintaining cardiovascular fitness. If it cannot be done continuously, exercise may also be performed in short bouts of ten to fifteen minutes two or three times a day.

- **Smoking**. Smoking is a deadly habit that has to be totally given up. Smoking is a cause of almost all cardiovascular illnesses in addition to nervous system illnesses like stroke and cancer. Quitting smoking is paramount in the prevention of CAD.

- **Diet**. Following a healthy diet is necessary. One must reduce the amount of fats in diet, especially the saturated variety of fat that is available in butter, *ghee*, lard etc. Lean meat is permissible. Egg consumption should be limited to one egg per day. Salt restriction is very important. Only about 5 grams of salt per day is permissible. This is equal to one teaspoonful of salt. It would be prudent to avoid adding salt on the table and keeping away from processed food where salt is a main ingredient. Also, pickles, wafers, fried chips and the like which are high in salt content are better avoided. Fruits and vegetables should form an important part of the diet and adequate fiber intake should be ensured. Whole grains should be included in the diet. Fish is quite good as the fish oils have a protective effect on the heart.

- **Co-morbidities**. In addition, diseases like Diabetes and High blood pressure should be properly treated and kept under control. Blood levels of cholesterol should be kept at the recommended levels.
- **Alcohol**. Alcohol consumption should be strictly controlled. Not more than two drinks a day for men and one drink for women, is recommended in the guidelines on alcohol consumption by the American Heart Association. One drink indicates, 12 oz of beer, or ale, 1.5 oz of whiskey, gin, vodka, or tequila, or 5 oz of red or white wine.
- **Stress management**. Managing stress goes a long way in ensuring a healthy life. Various methods of stress management are available like meditation, yoga, tai-chi, and others. Stress at home and at the work environment have to be properly addressed. As age advances, it is advisable to practice one of these stress management techniques to lead a calm and peaceful life.
- **Medical Checkup**. It is important to have an annual medical checkup after the age of 60. Any increase in blood pressure or serum cholesterol has to be treated as per the physician's advice. In the younger individuals, a checkup once in three years at least is mandatory if there is a family

history of heart disease. Any condition like heart failure, coronary artery disease or arrhythmia should be promptly treated.

HEART FAILURE

Heart failure (**HF**) is a condition where the muscles of the heart become weak, and the pumping capacity of the heart is reduced. So much so, the blood dams up in the heart and leads to various symptoms in the patient. Heart failure can be caused by various diseases of the heart. A heart attack damages part of the heart muscle and consequently the remaining muscle may not be able to pump blood forcefully resulting in heart failure. Diseases affecting the heart muscle (*Cardiomyopathy*), very high blood pressure, diseases of the heart valves, infections of the heart etc., can ultimately lead to heart failure.

What are the main symptoms of heart failure

- **Shortness of breath** on exertion is the most important symptom. Even minimal exertion like going to the toilet or having a bath produces severe breathlessness in these patients. Occasionally they have difficulty in breathing on lying down and this may be relieved when they sit up. Hence they may not be able to lie down flat at night and may have to sit up or propped up in bed. If an elderly patient has any of these symptoms or starts to cough and becomes short of breath on lying down, heart failure should be suspected.

- **Severe fatigue and exhaustion** may be noticed in these patients. Even a minor exertion may lead to severe fatigue. This is because the heart is not able to supply enough oxygen to the muscles and the rest of the body leading to severe tiredness and inability to exercise and take care of even one's day-to-day chores.

- **Swelling of the ankles, feet and legs** occurs in later stages of heart failure as fluid seeps from the small blood vessels into the tissues causing swelling of the dependent parts of the body like legs. The person may have puffiness of the face in the mornings after a night's sleep as the fluid may accumulate in the soft tissues of the face and around the eyes. When too much fluid accumulates in the tissues of the abdomen, there may be swelling of the belly. Owing to this, the patient's weight increases.

- **Cough** may be a prominent symptom of heart failure due to fluid collecting in the lungs. Occasionally this may be accompanied by pink frothy sputum which may be alarming.

- **Lethargy and drowsiness** in heart failure are due to the decrease in oxygen supply to the brain. Inability to concentrate or think properly may be seen. Reduced alertness is often present.
- **Other symptoms** of the underlying heart disease also may be seen like palpitations if the heartbeat is fast or irregular, chest pain if he has coronary artery disease or fever if there is an infection.

The patient with heart failure needs to be hospitalized to relieve the symptoms and once the condition improves, treatment at home would suffice. The patient will need support from the relatives and caregiver for his daily routine activities and must take his medications regularly. The treatment of heart failure is with medications which improve the performance of the heart and get rid of the excess fluid in the body. Oxygen inhalation is often needed in the patients. There are also medications which lessen the work of the heart.

Patients with heart failure should avoid crowded places and also be vaccinated against infections appropriately as advised by the physician. It is preferable for the elderly patient with heart failure to wear a mask when he is out of doors especially in a dusty or polluted environment.

HIGH BLOOD PRESSURE - HYPERTENSION

High blood pressure (**HBP**) is one of the commonest illnesses in elderly adults. Often it produces no symptoms by itself and a dangerous and life-threatening complication may be its first manifestation, Hence, it has been called the *'Silent killer'*.

When the heart pumps, the blood flowing into the blood vessels (arteries) exerts pressure on its walls. This is called blood pressure. Normally a certain amount of blood pressure is needed for the blood to flow forward in the blood vessels to keep the circulation going. When the blood vessels become stiffer in old age or due to other hormonal causes, the pressure in the blood vessels increases beyond normal. This is called High blood pressure or **Hypertension**.

When the heart contracts and pumps blood into the artery, the blood pressure inside the artery rises immediately. This is called the **Systolic blood pressure**. When the heart relaxes, the blood pressure in the artery decreases to a lower level and this is called the **Diastolic blood pressure**. Hence blood pressure reading is always given as two numbers, one higher (systolic) and one lower (diastolic). It is expressed in millimeters of mercury. The blood pressure in a normal person is 120-140 mm Hg systolic and 80 – 90 mm Hg diastolic. Values above these indicate high blood pressure.

What are the Risk Factors for HBP

There are many factors which can lead to the development of HBP in an individual. They are:

- **Age**. As age increases, the blood pressure also tends to rise.
- **Gender**. Generally, men have a higher blood pressure compared to women.
- **Family History.** High blood pressure tends to run in families and hence if one or both parents have HBP, the children have a higher chance of being affected when they reach adulthood.
- **Race**. African Americans also are at a higher risk of developing high blood pressure.
- **Diet**. A diet high in sodium (salt) and low in potassium poses a risk for

developing HBP. High salt is present in processed food and pickles. Potassium is available in foods like yoghurt, bananas, potatoes, coconut water, and beans.

- **Obesity and lack of exercise**. A healthy lifestyle is needed to avoid obesity. Regular exercise forms a part of a healthy lifestyle. A person who is obese and does not exercise regularly is at a higher risk of developing HBP.
- **Alcohol**. Excess consumption of alcohol may lead to high blood pressure and its complications. The daily consumption of alcohol has been defined previously.
- **Smoking**. Smoking increases the risk of developing high blood pressure. Nicotine has a blood pressure raising effect.

The Treatment of HBP rests on the two pillars of Medications and Lifestyle changes. The physician will prescribe appropriate medications for control of blood pressure depending on the patient's age and his other associated diseases. One has to be diligent in taking the medicine properly as advised.

Lifestyle changes as advised must be followed. Regular exercise, a prudent diet and other lifestyle changes as discussed previously. (See section on *Prevention of Coronary Artery Disease*).

Home monitoring of Blood Pressure.

Owing to the advances in technology, there are now instruments which have made measurement of blood pressure at home easy and convenient. The patients can self-monitor their blood pressure at home and keep a record of the readings. Electronic appliances are available now which are handy and easy to use.

However, the patient should never change or alter the dose of medications prescribed by the physician based on the home recordings. It should be done only on the advice of the treating physician.

What precautions one should remember while taking the medicines.

- As far as possible the medicines should be taken daily at the appropriate time prescribed by the physician.
- If the blood pressure recorded at home is too low or if symptoms like giddiness on standing up occur, the physician should be contacted to change the dose of the medication. The systolic blood pressure reading should not go below 100 mm of Mercury.
- The patient should not resort to 'self-medication' by altering the dose of medication by himself.

- The medication should never be stopped if normal blood pressure readings are obtained every time one takes the measurement. The blood pressure remains normal due to the medication and the dose should not be reduced or stopped by the patient. Any change in dose should be done only by the treating physician.
- It is helpful to remember the details regarding the medicines being taken and getting acquainted with their side effects.
- Whenever any other physician is seen for any other illness, the details of the medicines that the patient is presently taking should be given to him.

What complications can high blood pressure lead to?

High blood pressure can lead to complications which may be fatal. Hence it is important to keep blood pressure properly under control. The name 'Silent killer' is given to the disease because high blood pressure produces minimal or no symptoms but may kill the patient due to its complications. Hence it is important to be aware of the complications of high blood pressure.

- **Stroke** is a very important and dangerous complication of high blood pressure. It can be due to sudden bleeding into the brain due to bursting of a small blood vessel in the brain which is unable to withstand the high blood pressure. In many patients this could lead to a fatal outcome. Clotting of blood in a blood vessel in the brain also could be a consequence of high BP leading to a stroke. (See section on *Stroke*).

- **Kidney damage**. High BP when not properly treated or ignored can lead to kidney damage and ultimately to failure of the kidneys. This could be fatal.

- **Damage to the eyes.** The *retina* which is the screen of the eye on which the images which we see fall, is damaged by high BP leading to visual impairment and occasionally blindness.

- **Heart Diseases.** Enlargement of the heart, coronary artery disease causing heart attacks or sudden death can occur in HBP. Heart failure can occur as a complication of long standing HBP.

- **Aneurysms**. These are weak areas occurring in the walls of large arteries like the aorta due to the high blood pressure. This in turn cause the wall of the blood vessels to balloon out to form pouch like structures called *Aneurysms*. These can suddenly leak or burst causing torrential bleeding and prove immediately fatal.

- **Sexual dysfunction** like poor erection, and **cognitive decline** with subsequent dementia are also complications which can occur with HBP.

ATRIAL FIBRILLATION

Atrial fibrillation (**AF** or **AFIB**) is an irregularity of the heart beat caused by an abnormal heart rhythm. Abnormal rhythm of heart beat is named 'Cardiac Arrhythmia' in medical parlance. Atrial fibrillation is one such abnormal rhythm that tends to occur more frequently in old age. Atrial fibrillation implies that the atria, which are the upper chambers of the heart beat at a very fast and chaotic rate thereby causing the heart to beat irregularly and thereby impair the pumping of blood. Also, the irregular beating of the atria leads to blood damming up in those chambers and this can cause a blood clot to form which may dislodge from there and be carried into various parts of the body to cause blocking of the blood vessels. Thus, blocking of a blood vessel to the brain can lead to stroke in the patient or the clot may block a major artery to one of the patient's limbs. Hence atrial fibrillation is seen as a very dangerous heart rhythm needing urgent attention by the physician. Stroke is **five times** more common in patients with AFib than in those with normal heart rhythm.

Whereas AF prevalence is only 0.5% in those below the age of 40, in the elderly over 65 years, it rises to 5%. In those above 80 it is almost 10%. Various heart diseases can lead to this irregularity. Other causes of AF are High BP, Diabetes, and Thyroid disorders like an overactive thyroid gland.

The patient may present with symptoms of irregular palpitations or a 'fluttering' in the chest with or without pain, breathlessness, or dizziness. Some feel severe fatigue during these episodes of irregularity. These episodes may be intermittent initially and later on become permanently established. In most patients it may not cause any symptoms and may be accidentally detected by the physician on routine clinical examination as an irregularity of the patient's pulse. Alcohol can precipitate AF in certain individuals. Obesity, certain medications, and various heart diseases can be risk factors for causing AF.

The treatment of AFib consists mainly in controlling the fast heart rate and preventing clotting of blood within the heart. The physician gives medications which control the heart rate. Medications called *'Anticoagulants'* are prescribed so that the clots are prevented from forming inside the heart and being carried to various parts of the body like the brain leading to stroke. These medications have to be monitored with laboratory tests and the physician will advise the patient accordingly. Strict follow up with the doctor is needed in those patients taking anticoagulants.

Rarely interventional treatments or surgical measures may be advised by the physician to control the arrhythmia and to prevent clots from being carried out of the heart.

How can AF be prevented?

Prevention of AFib can be accomplished by the measures outlined for general prevention of heart diseases as given previously. Control of obesity, a healthy lifestyle, exercise, avoidance of smoking, reducing alcohol and coffee intake, controlling high blood pressure and diabetes, and keeping other diseases properly under control are important measures to prevent Atrial fibrillation.

Resources

1. Prevent heart disease – Centers for Disease control and prevention
2. High Blood Pressure – Centers for Disease Control and Prevention.

3. Heart Disease - Centers for Disease Control and Prevention. Atrial Fibrillation in the elderly. A review. FA Hakim & WA Shen. In Future Cardiology, Vol 10 No 6, 2014

4 Heart Failure - Centers for Disease Control and Prevention

5. Risk Factors for Coronary Artery Disease – Brown JC et al. March 2020

6.   Know your risk for high blood pressure.

7. Modifiable and Non-modifiable predisposing risk factors of myocardial infarction – A Review. Huma S et al. Journal of Pharmaceutical Sciences and Research. Vol 4. 2012, p 1649-1653.

8.   High blood pressure dangers : Hypertension's effects on your body.

Chapter 2. BRAIN & SPINAL CORD THE NERVOUS SYSTEM

Structure & Function. The presence of a complex brain distinguishes man from other creatures. The brain helps us to interact with the external world and at the same time helps us introspect, think, and solve problems.

The brain, the spinal cord and the nerves together constitute the **Nervous System.** The main unit of the nervous system is the nerve cell called the **Neuron.** Billions of neurons in the nervous system are interconnected with each other to form billions of interconnections called **Synapses.** Each neuron has one long branch or fiber called the **Axon.** These axons are bundled together to form **Nerves** which are distributed to the various parts of the body.

The nervous system consists of the **Central Nervous System (CNS)** which is made up of the brain and the spinal cord and the **Peripheral Nervous System (PNS)** which is made up of the various nerves.

In addition, there is an **Autonomic Nervous system (ANS)** composed of nerves which controls the various involuntary actions in the body like the gut muscles, secretory glands, heart rate, blood pressure, respiration, digestion, sexual arousal etc.

The nerves which carry signals from the brain and spinal cord to the peripheral organs and muscles are called **Motor Nerves**. Those that convey sensations like touch, temperature, and pain from various parts of the body to the CNS to be recognized are called the **Sensory Nerves**.

The nerve cells or neurons 'communicate' or send signals to each other through chemicals called **Neurotransmitters**. About 20 different chemicals have been identified which help in this transmission of signals.

Brain: The human brain is enclosed in the thick bony skull or **Cranium**. It weighs about 1.2 – 1.4 kg (2.6 to 3.1 lbs) in humans. It consists of three main parts. The two large, paired structures lying on both sides in the upper part of the brain are called the **Cerebral Hemispheres** or **Cerebrum**. They are connected to each other by a bundle of nerve fibers in the middle.

Below it is the **Brainstem** which appears like a stalk and this continues below as the **Spinal Cord**. The brain stem has three parts named the **Midbrain**, **Pons**, and the **Medulla**. Ten pairs of nerves arise from the brainstem to supply structures in the head and neck like the face, eye, ear, tongue etc. At the back of the brain is another smaller rounded structure called the **Cerebellum** meaning 'little brain' in Latin. **(See Fig.2)**

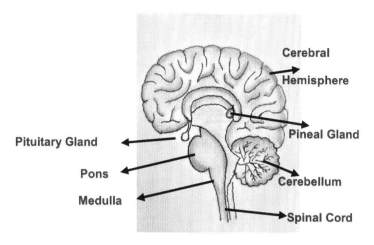

Figure 2 (Brain - Structure)

The brain and spinal cord are covered by three membranes called the **Dura mater, Arachnoid mater, and the Pia mater**. They protect the brain and spinal cord. Together these are named the '**Meninges'**.

The spaces between the meninges and the hollow spaces in the cerebral hemispheres and the brainstem and spinal cord are filled with a fluid called the **Cerebrospinal fluid** which acts as a water cushion for the brain and is also involved in its metabolism.

The blood supply to the brain is through four arteries, two on either side. They are branches of the Aorta and carry oxygenated blood and nutrients to the brain. They divide into smaller branches which penetrate into the brain to supply the whole interior of the brain.

The **Spinal Cord** is the long, thin, tubular structure encased within the vertebrae of the spine (backbone) and thus is well protected. It is a continuation of the lower part of the brainstem. It extends up to the lower part of the backbone.

Various nerves take off from the spinal cord at all levels and go to the different parts of the body.

The functions of the brain are numerous. The main function of the brain is to regulate the muscles and joints to perform voluntary movements. Involuntary movements like breathing, regulation of the blood pressure, beating of the heart, digestion, control of the bladder and bowels etc., are also under the control of the brain. The brain also receives and processes sensations like pain, temperature, touch, taste, smell, etc.

In addition, the brain is involved in higher functions like Memory, Language, Emotion, Speech etc.

The two cerebral hemispheres are concerned with the motor and sensory functions of the body. The cerebellum functions to fine tune the coordinated movements of the body and to maintain the balance of the body. The brainstem is involved in the involuntary movements already discussed and also controls of the muscles of the eye, hearing, face, and tongue.

The human brain controls man's movement, senses thoughts, and memories. The brain also controls the involuntary actions in our body like breathing, pumping of the heart, control of blood pressure, digestion of food in the gut etc. The nerves in the body are the conduits that carry the signals from the brain to various parts of the body and sensations from various parts of the body to the brain. The spinal cord encased in the rigid vertebral spine is the extension of the brain downwards and gives off many nerves that have various functions.

What happens to the brain when we age

Natural changes occur in the brain with aging. The brain shrinks with increase in age of the individual. After the age of 40 years the brain size and weight decreases by 5% per decade. This is due to the death of the nerve cells called Neurons. The number of nerve cells decreases. The nerve cells also become slow in processing information. Memory also decreases with age.

Neurological problems of old age may be gradual in onset or strike the individual like a bolt from the blue necessitating immediate admission to the hospital.

The gradual changes occurring in the elderly often get dismissed as part of aging and may not warrant a physician's attention. So much so, the diseases may not be recognized till it is far advanced.

However, it is important to recognize that there are changes in the individual with the advancing age which are normal and inevitable and hence may not need active intervention.

It is well recognized that after the age of 60 there is a decrease in the speed of conduction in the nerves. It has been reported that an elderly person with any three abnormal neurological signs has an increased mortality in the next ten years. So also, even minor neurological symptoms and signs may increase the chances of falls in elderly individuals. These facts should be considered while evaluating the elderly individual.

The common problems one encounters with the elderly are Delirium & Confusional states, Dementia and Alzheimer's disease, Strokes, Epilepsy in the elderly, Falls, and other minor ailments.

It has to be considered that some symptoms like difficulty in walking could be due to more than one factor or disease like muscle weakness, and disease of bones and joints also, and hence a multiple factors must be considered in diagnosing these conditions.

DELIRIUM & CONFUSIONAL STATES

Delirium and confusion are not uncommon in the elderly and may be associated with any medical illness. Occasionally minor medical illnesses like infections may cause delirium. It may be difficult to recognize and may be missed. Delirium has to be differentiated from **Dementia** which occurs gradually over a period of months or years. Delirium often indicates that there is some important and urgent medical problem that needs emergency management.

Delirium has been defined as *"an acutely disturbed state of mind that occurs in fever, intoxication, and other disorders and is characterized by restlessness, illusions, and incoherence of thought and speech"*. (Oxford Language Dictionary)

Delirium can present in elderly individuals in various ways

- Attention deficits like decrease in focus, decrease in awareness and shifting attention.
- Occasionally, it presents gradually over a few hours or even days. Delirium can fluctuate at times, giving a period of normalcy in between.
- Often, delirium can be caused by medical conditions like Pneumonia, fever due to any cause or even due to the side effects of some

medications being taken by the patient. One should also keep in mind that withdrawal symptoms due to alcohol and substance abuse can also present with features similar to delirium.

- In some individuals, delirium presents as increased activity or agitation and in others as reduced activity leading to lethargy and indifference.
- Variable emotional disturbances like fear, euphoria, confusion, inability to think clearly and coherently, decrease in attention span may all be signs of delirium in the elderly.

Confusion on the other hand indicates the *inability to think clearly at one's normal speed*. The person cannot think clearly or logically. The attention span may be reduced.

It is reported that about 30% of elderly patients develop delirium during hospital stay. It can also occur after complex surgical procedures and is called *'Post-surgical Delirium'*.

The more aged a person is, the more the chances of his developing delirium. If the person has already an underlying brain disease like Stroke, Dementia, or Parkinson's disease, the chances of delirium are increased.

There are some factors which may precipitate delirium in a vulnerable elderly individual.

- Multiple drugs especially that act on the brain like psychiatric medicines, sleeping tablets, antihistaminic medicines as used for common cold and in cough syrups can precipitate delirium in certain individuals.
- Acute infections like acute urinary tract infection, pneumonia, severe diarrhea.
- Low blood sugar or very high blood sugar in a diabetic may cause delirium.
- Abnormal levels of Sodium, Potassium, Calcium or Magnesium in blood can also present as delirium.
- Dehydration due to any cause. It may be due to inadequate intake of fluids by the elderly individual or may be due to increased loss of fluid from the body as in diarrhea or vomiting.
- Malnutrition due to inadequate food intake or intake of food without adequate nutritional supplements can also cause delirium.

What are the features of a person with delirium

Delirium often develops over a short period of time. It can fluctuate and at times the person may appear totally normal. He is not able to focus on any activity and often it is the members of the household or caregivers who note that the *'person is not behaving normally'*. He is easily distracted and may appear drowsy or lethargic. Some people exhibit agitation and may appear hypervigilant unlike their normal selves.

The individual may not be able to identify a close friend or relative or may misidentify the person. Objects in a room may be mistaken for a person like mistaking a coat in a hanger for a person standing near the wall. They also feel that others want to hurt them.

Persons with delusion often may not be able to speak in a second language in which they are well versed during normal behaviour. An Indian with Hindi as his mother tongue may not be able to speak in English even though he has learnt the language.

Delusion often develops over a period of hours or days. It may be short lived till the acute stage is over or the cause for the delirium is removed. However, it may last for days or months in rare cases.

It has to be kept in mind that delirium may be the only indication of a serious illness in an elderly individual. Heart failure, Pneumonia or severe urinary infection may present only as delirium and the primary cause for the delirium may be missed. Hence in any individual presenting with delirium, these causative factors should be looked for.

Agitation accompanies delirium in some individuals. They may be easily annoyed or do not want to be bothered. They prefer to be left alone. Lack of sleep may be a prominent symptom of delirium. They may feel irritable, anxious and may not tolerate loud sounds or bright light. They may show emotional disturbances seen as excessive crying or laughing.

A subtle change in the consciousness of the individual is often an early symptom which may be picked up by observant close relatives like the spouse or children. The delirious persons may not recognize where they are or indulge in 'nonsense talk'. The person may confuse day and night. They find it difficult in recalling events and show defects in memory, and an incoherent speech.

An interesting feature noticed in the behavior is called '*sundowning*'. Here the person exhibits a deterioration in his behaviour during evening hours even though they may be rather normal during the daytime. Though the cause for this is not fully known, it is seen more in persons with delirium and dementia and in those who are institutionalized.

Occasionally, a type of epilepsy without fits may also present just as delusion and confusion and mislead the attendant. The diagnosis of epilepsy may hence be missed.

There are some **Risk factors** that make a person more prone for delirium. They are :

- Age more than 70 years.
- History of delirium in the past.
- Vomiting or diarrhea due to any cause.
- Problems with impaired vision or hearing.
- Hospitalized patients, especially isolated in ICUs.
- A person taking five or more types of medications.

What complications can delirium cause

1. Delirium can increase the length of hospital stay. This in turn can lead to medical complications like bedsore, pneumonia, urinary infection etc.
2. Delirium can cause severe anxiety and fear in individuals.
3. Repeated attacks of delirium can cause a gradual deterioration in the mental abilities of the patient.
4. Patients with delirium often need full time care and may overburden the resources available and be troublesome to the near and dear ones.

How can we help an elderly person with delirium and confusion

i. Safe surroundings should be ensured for a delirious patient. There should not be excess noise or light in the room. Keep them calm.

ii. Talk to the delirious patient soothingly and use only simple phrases. Be sympathetic towards them.

iii. Encourage them to move about and sit in a chair instead of always lying in bed.

iv. Do not restrain them with any physical restrains if they are restless as this may lead to more confusion and aggravate the condition.

v. They have to be helped to eat and drink. Make sure that they consume adequate fluids.

vi. Request their friends and relatives to visit the patient so that they feel comfortable in their company.

vii. Soothing music, reading to them from books or scriptures may help them.

viii. Permit them to use their spectacles or hearing aids if they have been using them.

ix. Keep some familiar items in their room like their favorite pictures, pillows, clock etc.

x. Talk to them gently about the recent events, family news etc., to help orient them to the current situation. (Courtesy: Memorial Sloan Kettering Cancer Center)

STROKE

A **Stroke** or **Cerebrovascular accident** as is mentioned in medical parlance is *a sudden loss of brain function due to a disruption of blood supply to a part of the brain.* It is also called a '**Brain Attack**'. This is the main cardiovascular disorder seen in the United States. A stroke can lead to a temporary or permanent loss of function of the brain and is one of the most debilitating and disastrous of illnesses in the elderly. It leads to physical dependence on others for their daily activities and causes mental depression in many due to a feeling of helplessness. Hence in the elderly population, the aim should be to prevent a stroke rather than manage it after it occurs.

Stroke is the fifth cause of death in the 45 – 65 age group and is the third cause of death in those above 65 years of age. Stroke also is responsible for the high health cost incurred by the family and the healthcare system.

What are the Risk Factors causing Stroke

There are many Risk factors cause stroke. They can be roughly divided into the Non-Modifiable risk factors, which you cannot change and the Modifiable risk factors which you can alter with appropriate medical treatment or lifestyle modifications.

Non-Modifiable Risk Factors:

- Advanced age of over 55 years increases the risk of stroke in an individual.
- Males have a higher propensity for strokes compared to females
- Strokes are more common in the people of African American descent.

Modifiable Risk Factors:

- High Blood Pressure
- Smoking
- Diabetes mellitus
- Obesity
- Abnormal Heart Rhythms (Arrhythmias)
- Abnormal Blood levels of Fats (Lipids)
- Heart Disease

What causes Stroke?

Clotting of blood (*Thrombosis*) in one of the larger arteries supplying the brain is a major cause of an abrupt brain attack. Occasionally, smaller arteries supplying smaller areas of the brain may be involved leading to minor strokes causing relatively less *dysfunction* in the brain. Occasionally blood clots originating from elsewhere in the body, like the heart may be carried by the blood stream to lodge in one of the arteries of the brain leading to an abrupt stroke.

In some cases, instead of a clot in the artery of the brain there may be bleeding into the brain or outside the brain beneath its covering (meninges) causing compression of the brain due to a large clot. This can also present with symptoms similar to a stroke.

What are the Clinical Features of a patient with stroke?

This varies depending on the location of the damage to the brain, how extensive is the damage and how much blood is still able to reach the damaged area of the brain.

Hence the symptoms could vary depending on person to person. The main symptoms are due to malfunction of the brain and can present in various ways.

- Inability to move the limbs, usually in one half of the body is the most common presentation. Numbness and weakness occur in the face, arm, and leg on one half of the body. This is called **Hemiplegia** in medical terms.
- This may be associated with difficulty in speaking or in recognizing speech. Reading may be affected.
- There may be a change in the mental state of the patient and he may be confused. Delirium may be present.
- Gait may be affected and the patient may have loss of balance and tend to fall on standing or attempting to walk.
- Difficulty in swallowing may be present in some.
- Intense headache may be present in some patients.
- Another symptom seen is the presence of abnormal sensations in the body or parts of the body like pricking sensation, sensation of insects crawling etc. They may not be able to feel the sensation of touch or temperature or pain in the part affected.

What can a person do to prevent stroke?

Prevention of stroke should begin at an early age in adulthood. The most important advice to give any individual is to start following a healthy lifestyle from young age. It is not enough if the elderly follow the advice. Stroke prevention should start early in life when the person is healthy.

A healthy weight, preventing obesity, avoidance of smoking, regular exercise at least five days a week and a healthy nutritious diet go a long way in preventing stroke. In fact, the prevention of stroke is the same as the prevention of a heart attack as both are caused by similar risk factors. They are caused by almost by similar mechanisms in the brain and the heart respectively. (See section on *Coronary Artery Disease*)

Following the lifestyle advised above reduces a person's chances of getting a stroke by almost 50%. In addition, the public should be made aware of the condition and the relatives and caregivers should be aware of the early symptoms of stroke so that it can be recognized in the initial stages and early treatment instituted in a hospital to prevent progression of the stroke. Any sudden bizarre behaviour in an elderly or any mild symptoms pertaining to the nervous system should be given due importance and attended to immediately.

How would you care for a patient with stroke at home?

Patients with stroke often get depressed owing to their inability to perform their normal day to day functions. They need help, but the caregiver should be careful to encourage self-help in them and not do everything for them. Some of the important points to remember are:

- Encourage the patient to <u>exercise and walk about</u>. They will need the help of a walking stick or a walker. But persistence pays and they must learn to walk independently over a period of time.
- Be on the lookout for any <u>new symptoms of stroke</u> that may develop and inform the doctor immediately. Any change in the person's status for the worse should immediately be brought to the notice of the treating doctor.
- Recovery after stroke often tends to stabilize and reach a steady state after three or four months. The patient should be encouraged to keep on trying to attain normalcy. The caregiver should <u>motivate the patient</u> to keep on trying and pushing them without permitting them to slow down their activities. A gentle coercion is needed in this regard.

- One must be careful to avoid falls in patients with stroke as even a minor fall may result in a setback to recovery.
- Modifications around the house may have to be made wherever needed to prevent falls, as the risk of a fall after a stroke is much higher compared to that of a normal elderly person. Grab bars in the rest room, non-slip mats, reduction of clutter in the rooms, proper positioning of furniture etc., go a long way in helping them. (Refer section on *"Falls in the Elderly"*)
- In the acute stages of stroke when the patient is bedridden, extreme care is needed to prevent bedsore and pressure on nerves which could lead to paralysis of the nerves. Also, lying in the same posture for a long time may lead to the muscles becoming stiff leading to permanent contractures of the muscles and the limbs may assume abnormal positions. To avoid these, the patient's posture should be frequently changed and his limbs should be passively moved by the caregiver at regular intervals. Occasionally splints will have to be provided to keep the limbs in extended positions especially during night. This will prevent contractures of the muscles.
- The patient will need physical therapy with the help of a therapist. The caregiver also should be familiar with the exercises prescribed for the patient. The exercises

should be broken down into multiple short periods of supervised exercises as the patients tend to tire easily.

- Ensuring <u>personal hygiene</u> for the patient is of extreme importance as soiling of the clothes and skin should be avoided. The skin around the private parts should be kept clean and dry always and tight-fitting undergarments must be avoided. Undergarments should be made of cotton and not of synthetic material. Males should be assisted to stand while passing urine. Post breakfast toilet should be encouraged to develop a routine habit daily.

- Frequent <u>inspection of the skin</u> of the patient especially around the bony points like shin, elbow, hip, shoulders should be done to detect any redness or soreness early as this may be the harbinger of a bedsore. The skin should always be kept dry. Applying a few drops of coconut oil and massaging has been found effective in preventing bedsores.

- Early in the treatment phase, <u>speech therapy</u> may be started with the help of a speech therapist. The patient should be encouraged to speak frequently or read aloud if they are able to do so.

- When the patient starts to walk, balancing the body will be a challenge in the early stages and <u>exercises for improving balance</u> must be encouraged. Assisted walking

- should be encouraged. Assistive devices to help walking should be used.
- Patients with stroke often are emotionally labile and tend to get depressed and irritable. They may be given to sudden bouts of laughing or crying. They may get depressed or anxious. <u>Empathy and emotional support</u> is needed in caring for them. The caregiver has to be sensitive to their reactions. One should talk to them taking care to speak slowly so that they understand the caregiver. When giving directions, care should be taken to give them only one instruction at a time.
- The patients should be taught and encouraged to take care of themselves. For this various <u>assist devices</u> are available. An occupational therapist will be helpful in planning this. The patient should be encouraged to participate in recreational activities or hobbies whenever they can. They should be encouraged to interact with friends and members of the family. Pets may give them a special motivation. Be careful to avoid social isolation in the patient.
- <u>Cognitive and perceptual re-training</u> will be needed with the help of a therapist in these patients and they will have to be encouraged to return to normal life as early as possible.

- Of course, any <u>associated medical problems</u> of the patient like diabetes, high blood pressure, high blood cholesterol etc., should be managed appropriately with the help of the attending physician.
- All the patient's <u>medical documents</u> should be kept organized. There are support groups available for the stroke patients and their help could be taken.

What home modifications may be needed for stroke patients

Home improvements will be helpful for stroke patients to assist them to live independently and prevent falls and other accidents. The home should be made stroke-friendly for the patient. Simple measures often help but occasionally major modifications may be needed in the home especially in those living independently. Even though these amenities may be available in the assisted living community, often patients tend to opt for living in their familiar surroundings and in the comfort of their home. Relatives too may prefer their near and dear ones to live with them in their sunset years. This is more so in the Asian countries where taking care of the elderly is part of the inherent culture.

The home modifications help to make life easy for them and help them to return to normal life. It also makes their life safe and independent.

Some of the modifications which may be helpful are as follows:

- Railings and grab bars can be provided in the bathrooms near the toilet and the shower. They may also be useful near the bed, stairs etc. Raised toilet seats or bedside commodes with or without arm rests may be provided so that getting on and off them becomes easier. Soap dispensers in the bathroom are better than soap bars or tubes.
- The patient should be advised not to lock the bathroom/toilet door.
- Door knobs may be replaced with handles or door-knob-extenders to make manipulation easy.
- Shower hoses (hand-shower) may be provided so that they can sit on a stool while showering.
- Non slip bath mats should be provided in the bathrooms and toilets.
- Rug-grippers may be fixed under the rugs to prevent slippage or sliding of the rugs when the patient is using the walker or the walking stick. Non slip adhesive pads are available which can be used under the rugs and carpets.

- Walking areas should be kept clear of clutter and loose wires should not be left lying on the floor.
- Ramps may be provided in the home especially if the patient is wheelchair bound.

These are some of the modifications that may be made in the home to ease the life of the patient with stroke.

What are the residual effects of stroke

Stroke leaves different residual effects on different people depending on the extent of damage to the brain and the site of damage in the brain. The commonest effect is paralysis of one half of the body called Hemiplegia. It is in the side opposite to the damage in the brain. When the left side of the brain is damaged, the right side of the body is affected.

The muscles may exhibit stiffness, called **spasticity** which decreases their range of movement. If this is left unmanaged, over a period of time, the muscles contract permanently leading to shortening of the muscles and the limb assuming grotesque postures. This has to be prevented by regular physical therapy and by splinting the limbs if needed.

Some persons with stroke exhibit fatigue and excess sleepiness during day time. The individual may not be able to balance himself and feels unsteady on standing and walking. This has to be overcome by physical therapy and special exercises for maintaining balance.

If the muscles are not adequately exercised, for a long period of time they decrease in bulk leading to severe weakness . This is called **atrophy**. Weakness of the muscles in the throat can lead to swallowing difficulties in some. This can be set right by training with a swallowing specialist.

Other effects on cognition may be very important. Difficulty in speaking and language are common in those where the left side of the brain in damaged in a stroke. Various types of speech disorders can occur. They can be effectively treated by adequate training with a speech therapist.

Impaired memory, reduced attention span, impairment of thinking, confusion, reduced attention span, emotional lability, changes in behavior like aggressive behavior, depression and anxiety may be the residual effects seen in some patients. These can be reduced to a large extent by working with a physical therapist trained in the management of these conditions.

When certain parts of the brain involved in the sensory function are damaged, the patient may experience various abnormal sensations. Numbness, loss of sensation in some parts of the body, visual disturbances, or severe pain in some parts of the body called 'Post stroke pain syndrome' may occur in some.

In an acute setting of stroke various medical complications can occur. These are preventable by adequate measures and good nursing care. Bedsores, incontinence due to inadequate control of the bladder and the bowels, pneumonia occasionally caused by food entering the windpipe during swallowing of solids or liquids, clotting of blood in the veins of the lower limbs due to inadequate exercise, and frequent headaches may all occur as complications of stroke. They have to be anticipated and prevented adequately.

The caregiver of a patient with stroke needs to approach the patient with sympathy and lots of patience as mood swings are possible in these individuals. Furthermore, the caregiver should be aware of all the medications that the patient is on and their side effects. Even a minor setback or a minor fall or slipping should be taken seriously and measures to avoid it should be taken immediately.

MEMORY LOSS AND AGING

It is common knowledge that aging causes some degree of memory loss. The elderly get upset when they cannot recollect names of persons or places. Often they do not remember the recent events. They may not remember what they had for dinner the night before. These events which seem apparently normal to the young, may create anxiety and a feeling of helplessness and insecurity in the elderly individual. They may forget to renew a magazine subscription or to pay a pending telephone bill. While speaking to their kith and kin they may not get the appropriate word or may forget the name of an object. They misplace things like keys, mobile phone, spectacles, wallet etc. and forget where they kept them. They may forget items in a grocery list. They may not be able to learn a new skill easily. In these modern days, learning to use a smart phone often foxes them. These situations of 'forgetfulness' are often a part of normal aging and do not always indicate a serious memory problem. These are manageable and do not affect their social life or work. Thus, forgetting things once in a while can be considered as part of the normal aging process and the elderly should be reassured about this.

But serious problems involving the cognitive function have to be view with concern. ***Cognitive function*** *includes thinking, remembering, learning, and reasoning.*

However, when memory loss begins to affect day to day activities and a person's normal life, it has to be taken seriously and medical help sought. If the memory loss begins to affects daily activities like driving, speaking on the phone or finding one's way home, then it indicates a more serious illness.

When will you take your elderly relative to the physician?

There are some situations and symptoms that warrant medical attention at the earliest opportunity.

- If the person gets lost in places which he or she knows very well like returning from the grocer's shop or from a close friend's or relative's house.
- If the person tends to get confused about the time, date, place, or people whom they meet.
- If they keep repeating a question over and over again.

- If they find difficulty in following clearly given directions.
- If they are not properly caring for themselves like eating properly, bathing or exhibiting behaviour which is unsafe.

Mild Cognitive Impairment is defined as "*cognitive decline greater than expected for an individual's age and education level but that does not interfere notably with activities of daily life*". Here the deterioration in thinking and memory are minimal compared to individuals of the same age. The person is otherwise normally active and functions in society and in his work without significant problems. The changes are subtle and may be seen as losing things often, forgetting appointments or fumbling for words or names. Usually, it is not of much issue, but may be a harbinger of dementia or even more serious illness like Alzheimer's disease.

What are the reversible causes of memory loss ?

There are some conditions which produce memory loss or cognitive decline which can be reversed by appropriate treatment. Hence it becomes imperative that they are not missed. The reader should be aware of these conditions so as not to stamp the changes in a loved one as permanent. A physician who treats dementia can check for these conditions clinically or using various tests. However, it is incumbent on the relatives to know about these conditions so that they can be recognized and appropriate advice sought at the correct time.

1. <u>Hypothyroidism.</u> A decrease in the secretion of hormones by the thyroid gland can produce symptoms resembling depression and memory impairment. (See section on *Endocrine Diseases-Hypothyroidism)*

2. <u>Emotional Disorders.</u> Stress, anxiety, and depression may present with forgetfulness, confusion, mild cognitive impairment, and inability to concentrate. This improves with treatment of the basic condition.

3. <u>Vitamin B12 Deficiency.</u> This is an important vitamin, the deficiency of which can mimic dementia or Alzheimer's disease. Vegetarians and the elderly are prone for this deficiency and it could be due to poor nutritional intake.

4. <u>Minor head injury.</u> Occasionally a minor head injury may be ignored and may lead to a temporary state of memory impairment.

5. <u>Medications.</u> In the elderly certain medications can trigger delirium or a transient memory impairment compared to the younger individuals. This has to be kept

in mind when caring for the elderly on multiple medications.

6. <u>Alcoholism</u>. Chronic alcoholism can impair memory either due to the damage to the brain caused by the alcohol intake or to associated nutritional deficiencies like Vitamin B1 (thiamine) deficiency.

7. <u>Other causes.</u> Other causes such as diseases of the brain like Tumors, infections, depression, sleep disorders or normal pressure hydrocephalus- a condition where extra fluid gets trapped in the brain causing the pressure inside the skull to rise.

What can one do to prevent and improve loss of memory?

There are many recommendations for preventing loss of memory in old age. It is important for individuals entering the sixth and seventh decades of life to start practicing these to ward off the memory changes that may occur with increasing age. Some of the methods to prevent and improve memory are as follows:

- <u>Regular exercise</u> at least five times a week lasting 30 to 45 minutes a day is an important component of prevention. Lifestyle diseases like Diabetes, high blood pressure, obesity, high blood cholesterol are risk factors for developing memory impairment and these can be controlled to a large extent by adequate exercise. Simple noncompetitive exercises like Yoga, Tai-chi and other low impact exercises may be done by the elderly without straining their joints. Cycling, swimming, and brisk walking are easy and doable. For those who cannot exercise continuously for half an hour, ten or fifteen minutes of walking two or three times a day would be a good alternative.

- A healthy diet should supplement the exercise regimen. Increased consumption of fruits and vegetables are very important. Lean proteins, whole grains, berries, lean poultry, fish, beans, and the inclusion of olive oil in diet are salutary to good mental health and memory.

- Lifestyle diseases like high blood pressure, diabetes, and high blood cholesterol should be controlled with medications on the advice of a physician. Medications should be regularly taken. The elderly may be provided pill boxes to ensure that they do not forget to take their medications.

- Adequate sleep should be ensured as it gives rest to the brain and restores and consolidates one's memories. The presence of sleep disturbances increases the chances of depression and anxiety. At least 7 to 9 hours of restful sleep should be ensured for the elderly.

- <u>Reading and learning</u> some new skill or language should be done daily to keep one's mind engaged. Playing games like chess and indulging in solving crossword puzzles and number games like Sudoku, stimulate the mind and keep it active and alert. These help to reduce the chances of memory impairment. Trying creative writing like essays, stories or poetry will go a long way in jogging one's mental abilities and provide a stimulus to memory. The elderly can be encouraged to tell stories to young children to exercise the mind and boost their memories.
- <u>Social isolation</u> is a risk that the elderly should avoid. They should mingle with individuals in society and engage in activities that keep them engaged. They should seek to spend more time with their loved ones and friends. Joining a club or a religious community where group activities are done, volunteering for social activities, and engaging in outings are some activities that keep them active. They can volunteer in schools to tell stories to children or read books to them. Volunteering in hospices to read to the bedridden or to keep them company for conversation, learning a musical instrument for the first time, driving through different routes while going out, to avoid the monotony are some

methods one can choose to keep the mind active and alert.

- <u>Smoking</u> is absolutely prohibited. <u>Alcohol</u> should be used to a minimum or totally shunned. Only low alcohol beverages like wine or beer should be taken.

- <u>Being Organized</u> is very important. They should aim to keep their home without clutter. To remember dates and other matters, they should write down what they have to do for the day. Keep a record of what to do daily. Reminders to pay bills, keep appointments, visit the doctor, renew a deposit etc., may be kept in calendars, diaries, in an electronic planner, the mobile phone or in a whiteboard on the wall of the room. Whenever needed, the 'Google assistant' can be asked to help. Relatives and caregivers also can make a daily list for the individuals.

- <u>Avoiding multitasking</u> is very important in the elderly. This can confuse them. Distractions should be kept to a minimum.

- <u>Having a fixed place for things</u> like keys, cards, check books, wallet, spectacles, wrist watch, pens etc., should be made a habit so that the person remembers where to look for it. Keeping these in a basket is more useful. The person should make it a point to make a daily routine and stick to this routine as much as possible.

ALZHEIMER'S DISEASE

Any discussion on memory impairment would be incomplete without a discussion on Alzheimer's disease (**AD**). *"Alzheimer's disease is a brain disorder that slowly destroys memory and thinking skills and, eventually, the ability to carry out the simplest tasks"* (National Institute on Aging). The disease progressively destroys memory and thinking skills. It is named after Dr. Alois Alzheimer who described the disease in 1906 in a woman who died of such symptoms. It is one of the commonest memory impairing diseases. It is progressive and irreversible.

On an average, 10-15% of individuals with mild cognitive impairment progress to develop Alzheimer's disease. Approximately 6.5 million Americans have AD as estimated in 2022. By 2050 it is projected to increase to 12.7 million. These staggering figures emphasize the importance of diagnosing the disease early. The statistics are mind boggling. About 1 in 9 Americans above the age of 65 have AD. About two-thirds of the patients are women and the

Afro Americans have almost double the incidence. Once diagnosed, the survival is about four to eight years. (Courtesy: The Alzheimer Association).

How to detect AD early? What are the symptoms?

The disease is often relentless and progressive. It affects memory, reasoning and thinking. Often it starts insidiously to progress to more severe forms. The symptoms may be summarized as follows.

- **Daily activities**. Forgetting information learnt recently is often the common symptoms. Important dates and events may be forgotten by the individual. He may repeat the same question multiple times to the relatives or caregivers. The person has to resort to memory aids like notes repeatedly or rely on family members to remember things.
- **Numbers**. The individual finds difficulty in dealing with numbers. They may find it difficult to keep track of the monthly bills, manage their bank accounts or plan something which they could do easily previously. They also take a longer time to perform these tasks unlike before.
- **Daily tasks**. Common tasks of daily living like driving, writing a grocery list, dressing, planning a simple event etc., may

take more time or become difficult for the person.

- **Time and Place**.   The person may not be able to remember the day of the week or the dates. They may also forget where they are at present.
- **Visual images**.   They find it difficult to read. Balance may become a problem and they tend to sway while walking. They find it difficult to appreciate various shades of colors and while driving, they get confused in judging distances.
- **Conversation**.   Patients with AD have trouble conversing with others. They may abruptly stop talking while continuing a conversation with others or fumble for words. They may name objects wrongly like a table as a cot or a cup as a bottle.
- **Misplacing objects**.   These individuals may place things in unusual and inappropriate places like leaving the keys in the refrigerator or placing shoes in the table drawers. Often they tend to lose things and since they forget where they kept them, may even accuse others of pilfering their belongings.
- **Judgement**.   The AD patient finds it difficult to handle money and makes poor judgement while dealing with their funds. They do not pay any attention to grooming themselves or keeping clean. Often they do not bathe regularly and may wear their

clothes in the wrong manner or shoes in the wrong legs. They find it difficult to make decisions. They are unable to make proper judgements.

- **Moods & Personality**. Their moods often keep on fluctuating and they may become depressed or anxious. They may become suspicious of others and feel that others want to harm them. They become fearful and confused. Even simple matters easily upset them.

- **Late stages**. In the moderate and severe stages of the disease, the person tends to have severe memory loss and confusion. They may fail to recognize their immediate family members and close friends. Restlessness, difficulty in sleeping, personality changes and the possibility of wandering off by themselves and getting lost may occur. They may develop urinary and fecal incontinence and need help for personal care. They find eating food difficult due to chewing and swallowing problems. They are unable to sit or stand or walk by themselves and need help for everything.

How to care for a patient with AD

Gentle supportive care is needed in managing these persons. They are dissociated from reality in later stages of the disease and are not aware of their surroundings or relatives. They seem to be in a world of their own. Daily living is a burden for them and they will have to be assisted for their daily needs. The caregiver should be compassionate and empathetic. One must be patient while dealing with these individuals.

- **Safety**. Keeping the AD patient safe from accidents and self-harm is one of the most important parts of managing them. They have a high risk of falling. Their walking shoes should be properly fitting and comfortable. Their room should be kept uncluttered and free of loose objects on the floor. Rugs or carpets should be fixed properly or removed. Edges of furniture may need padding if they are sharp. As far as possible, they should not be given plates, cups and other crockery made of glass or other breakable materials. The water temperature for bathing should be checked before they bathe. Their closets or drawers may have to be labelled so that they recognize them. As far as possible, their medications should be handed to them by a caregiver. They should not be permitted to take the medications by themselves as they may forget having taken them and repeat the dose leading to medication overdose. Pill boxes for daily medications may be used in the early stages of the disease when the patients are able to care for themselves. Driving should not be allowed when the disease progresses. Walking aids like canes or walkers may be needed according to the need. Items like medicine cabinets, alcohol, toxic household cleaners and detergents, hazardous chemicals, firearms, and tools should be kept away from them, locked if necessary to prevent accidental self-harm. So also, they should not have access to matches or cigarette lighters.

- **Daily Routine**. It is ideal to follow a fixed daily routine. The patient should be tuned in to this routine and follow it diligently. Any abrupt changes in this routine should be avoided as far as possible because this may confuse them and make them more aggressive or depressed. It is appropriate to keep them engaged in minor activities of cooking. This should be done under supervision of a relative or caregiver so that they do not harm themselves at the stove, or with electrical equipment or knives. They should be involved in simple non-strenuous daily chores around the house like folding the laundry, making the bed, setting the table, and helping in the garden. They should be taken outside for a walk and encouraged to exercise. Going to the park, museum, or zoo provides adequate exercise and keeps them active. They should be taken to visit friends and relatives. The relatives and friends should also be encouraged to visit the patient frequently and keep them company. They should be encouraged to watch movies along with the other family members. They should be involved with the family members and never feel isolated. This increases their self-esteem.

- **Communication**. AD affects a person's ability to communicate. The person may suddenly stop talking and lose his ability to communicate during mid-sentence. When talking to them, the caregivers and family members should always make eye contact with the patient and ask questions only one at a time or tell them only one point at a time. Keep the questions or instructions simple. They may not understand complex instructions. Call the persons by name whenever you speak to them. Always speak to them slowly and softly without raising the voice. Be careful to talk to them calmly even if they lose their temper or become angry or irritable.

- **Diet and Nutrition**. The caregivers and family members should ensure that the person takes food properly and remains well hydrated. At least 8 – 10 glasses of fluid including water, coffee, juices, and liquid food like porridge or *conjee* should be consumed by them daily. Often they tend to forget that they have eaten already or what they ate. Gently remind them. They may not be aware of the time for lunch or dinner. Their smell and taste may also be impaired and they may refuse to eat. They may complain regarding the taste of the food. In addition, trouble with chewing and swallowing may complicate the situation. Be careful to serve the food to them at the same time daily and use colorful plates and crockery whenever possible. Some food items will have to be cut into smaller pieces for them to eat easily e.g., fruits, cheese, sandwiches, bread, pancake etc. As far as possible, choose easily chewable and semi solid but nutritious food for them. Keep the dining area noise free. Avoid the TV, radio or loud music during eating. Take care to eat with them so that they do not feel lonely. A tablet of multivitamin may be given on the recommendation of your physician.

- **Hygiene**.   The patients with AD should be helped and encouraged to look after themselves. They should be told to brush their teeth at least twice daily. Men should be encouraged to shave themselves as long as they can do it safely. They must be helped to groom themselves and take care of their dental hygiene. Women should preferably avoid eye makeup. Simple make up may be permitted if they can do it themselves. Often the patients will be clumsy while they dress. One must patiently allow themselves to dress up. Buttoning up may be difficult for some and may need help. As far as possible, allow the patient to choose the dress that he wants to wear. Instead of buttons, the dresses may be provided with Velcro or zippers for ease of wear. Remind them to wash hands before eating and always after using the toilet. They tend to forget these minor hygienic practices. Their nails must be kept trimmed and they may need help doing that.

- **Pets**.   The patients with AD need not be deprived of their pets as far as it is safe for them. Pets like cats and dogs can provide companionship to them and often the patients enjoy the company of pets. So also, allow children to mingle with them and encourage them. It is preferable for an adult to supervise these activities.

- **Activities**.   Their daily activities should be flexible whenever needed. For example, they can be asked whether they want to go for a walk or would rather have a bath at that time. They could be given a set of two or three dresses and asked to choose one. They should be encouraged to participate in the activities and chores around the home along with others. Simple and direct instructions should be given to them. Patience is needed for the family members and the caregiver as these patients tend to take more time in performing any task.

- **Medications**. The advice of the medical practitioner should be followed and they should be given the medications regularly at the prescribed intervals. If unable to swallow, the tablets may be crushed and administered with food like porridge or with honey. (See section on *Swallowing-ENT*) They should be vaccinated against diseases like Influenza, Pneumonia and Covid.

- **Use of Technology & Support system**. Now a days a variety of smart home devices are available like voice commands to play music, control the lighting in the house or change the temperature. Automatic pill dispensers are available which alert the user when it is time to take the medications. The patient may be given trackers or locator devices in their keys, wallet, or their smart phone so that the household members can know where they are. The Google assistant can be put to good use to remind them of the daily chores. The patient should be given an identity tag with his name, diagnosis, and necessary contact information.

FALLS IN THE ELDERLY

Falls are common in the elderly. It is a major hazard in those who live independently. A Fall is defined as *"a person coming to rest on the ground or another lower level"*. WHO has defined "Elderly" as those above the age of 65, whereas the United Nations has defined age above 60 as "Older Population" or "Old Age".

In the community the incidence of falls in the elderly approximately is 30 – 40% whereas in Nursing homes it is approximately 50 – 60%. In one study from the US, 27.5% of those over the age of 65 reported at least one fall in the past year, 10.2% had fall related injuries and it was noticed that 34% of the falls were in those above the age of 85. Falls are more common in women compared to men. It is noted that 60% of persons have recurrent falls.

WHO reports that approximately 684000 individuals die from falls globally of which over 80% are in low- and middle-income countries. Each year about 37.3 million falls that are severe enough to require medical attention occur. Worldwide, falls are the second leading cause of accidental deaths due to injury.

Falls are the Primary cause of accidental death in the elderly and several factors are identified for the same. Evidence based investigations have proved that falls are preventable if proper action is taken in time. Applying preventive measures in the vulnerable population impacts public health. Almost 50% of the falls are recurrent.

Impairment of many of the systems of the body are the cause for the falls. Problems with the nervous system, bones, joints, muscles, or heart can lead to falls. Occasionally, the falls are minor not causing any serious impairment and hence the patient may not reveal it to anybody. There may not be any injury at the time of the fall. But not uncommonly, a minor fall with an injury to the head, even if trivial could lead to a serious condition called 'Subdural Hematoma' where blood clots outside the brain and compresses the brain. (See Complications of Falls) The morbidity like fractures and sprain due to the falls is more common than death caused by the falls.

Falls may result in minor or major injuries and complications resulting from falls are the fifth leading cause of death in those over the age of 65. In the elderly 95% of the hip fractures are caused by falls. It is more common in those who live alone. The fear of falls, consequently restricts the activities of such individuals.

What are the factors that could cause falls in the elderly

For purpose of convenience, let us divide these causes into three.

1. Intrinsic factors. These are factors related to the individual patient like medications taken by the patient which may cause dizziness, diseases of the patient like muscle or joint diseases etc.
2. Extrinsic factors. Environmental hazards like uneven surface, slippery surface, new home, unsafe stairways, slippery bath, mats, carpets etc.
3. Situational factors. Related to activities like walking while talking on the phone, being distracted during multitasking, failing to notice a step or curb, or rushing to the bathroom at night, rushing to answer the phone, walking in the presence of poor lighting etc.

Risk Factors and Causes for a Fall

Several risk factors which can cause a fall in the elderly have been recognized.

1. <u>History of previous falls</u>. A person who had a fall once has more chances of repeated falls.
2. <u>Balance impairment</u>. Aging itself causes some impairment of balance in the individual. Along with this if they have any illnesses that impair balance like diseases of the ear or nervous system, the chances of a fall are more.
3. <u>Decreased muscle strength</u>. Decrease in the muscle bulk and strength occur with aging. This is a normal phenomenon. Regular exercises to a large extent prevent this. Nervous system diseases like Stroke and Parkinson's disease also make an individual prone for falls.
4. <u>Visual Impairment</u>. Impairment of vision in the elderly is common. It could be due to cataract or other diseases of the eye. This could lead to falls in them.
5. <u>Polypharmacy</u> When more than 4 drugs are given to the patient or when Psychiatric drugs and drugs causing sedation are given.
6. <u>Gait impairment and walking difficulty</u>. This can occur when there are diseases of the joints or bones. It can also occur in certain diseases of the nervous system.
7. <u>Orthostatic Hypotension</u>. When the patient stands erect, the blood pressure decreases slightly and causes less blood to flow to the brain causing dizziness or transient loss of consciousness. This is called Orthostatic

Hypotension. It is known that 5 – 25% of the elderly may have a fall in blood pressure on standing at some time or the other. It can occur due to various causes like long standing Diabetes resulting in weakness of the nervous system, *dehydration*, Parkinson's disease, some medications, and various endocrine diseases. This condition should be recognized and appropriate measure adopted for its prevention. Prolonged standing is to be avoided in old age like standing in queues.

8. <u>Age over 80</u> years doubles the risk of falling.
9. <u>Female sex</u>, especially the obese, have an increased risk of falling.

   10. <u>Incontinence</u> of Urine or stools leading to hurrying to the toilet is often one cause of falls.

11. Any <u>acute or chronic pain</u> in the patient may cause a sudden tendency to fall when getting up from the bed or a chair.
12. <u>Diseases of the heart</u> can also lead to falls if the patient has sudden palpitations due to bouts of irregular heart beat or a very slow heart rate. The blood pressure too can decrease suddenly in patients who have heart diseases and cause sudden falls.
13. <u>*Dehydration*</u>, often due to inadequate intake of fluids by the elderly may be an important cause of falls in the elderly.

14. Alcohol intake in the elderly, if not curtailed also can be a cause of falls.
15. Improper footwear is also an important risk factor leading to falls. Shoes with thin hard soles are the best for balance and lower the risk of falls. Athletic shoes or sneakers are ideal. Walking barefoot or with socks alone is a risk for falling. Wearing high heels poses the greatest risk in women.

Complications of a fall in the Elderly

This depends on the situation and the amount of injury to the patient and the site of injury. Bruises, Sprains, and fractures of bones are the commonest of the injuries. However, there may be other serious injuries also.

- A fall which may go unrecognized or ignored may later produce effects on the brain due to blood clotting on the brain's outer surface under the covering of the brain called the *dura mater*. It is called **Chronic Subdural Hematoma** and the symptoms often occur late after days or weeks. The person may not even remember the event which caused the injury. It is often due to a trivial injury to the head which at the time of injury produces no symptoms and may go unrecognized. Injuries as trivial as bumping one's head against the door post or on a refrigerator door, slipping and hitting one's head against a piece of furniture are some of the causes that may later lead to a chronic subdural hematoma. The symptoms may be variable with headaches leading to difficulty in walking, weakness of limbs, occasionally epilepsy like seizures, difficulty in speech and writing, memory impairment, confusion, and coma. This condition is eminently curable by immediate surgery to remove the blood clot and hence should be diagnosed by a physician. *The relatives or care giver of the elderly should be aware of this condition and if they notice any change in the behaviour or general wellbeing of the individual who has had a minor trauma to the head previously, this condition should be suspected and immediate medical help sought.*

- Fracture of major bones like the hip bone, thigh bone or the bone of the arms, forearms or wrist are other complications resulting from falls.
- Serious falls may cause injury to the spine and any injury to the spine in the neck could lead to serious issues like paralysis.
- Chronic pain or discomfort may be present for a long time after a fall in most elderly individuals.
- Falls may lead to prolonged immobility due to confinement in bed caused by fractures. These could lead to various medical

complications like bedsores, pneumonia, incontinence of urine and feces.

- Following a fall, a person may have difficulty in moving around unaided for a long time and may need assistance to do so or seek the help of assistive devices.
- Falls lead to a decrease in the quality-of-life, financial costs of hospitalization increase, social isolation may occur.
- Anxiety, depression, frustration, fear of falling repeatedly are all consequences of falls which the elderly have to bear.
- Though uncommon death may be a complication of falls. The death rate due to falls reported by the CDC is 65 per 100,000 population of older adults. Death rate due to falls in those over 65 years of age rose by 30% between 2009 and 2018. The WHO reports that approximately 684 000 individuals die from falls globally of which over 80% are in low- and middle-income countries.

What can be done to prevent falls in the elderly

- A regular check-up with the family physician or any other doctor will be helpful in making an early diagnosis of any condition in the elderly that could lead to a fall. Medications and their dosage also could be adjusted if the individual has a regular follow up with his physician.

- An elderly individual should also be encouraged to keep moving and perform light exercises. Regular physical activity prevents falls to a great extent. Gentle exercises such as walking, Tai-chi, swimming etc., are good exercises that could be recommended. Exercise increases strength, co-ordination, balance, and flexibility.

- The elderly should be encouraged to wear shoes instead of slippers. Footwear should be sensible and fit properly. It should be anti-skid and prevent falls. Proper footwear also reduces joint pains by relieving the strain on joints of the legs.

- Any home hazards that could pose a threat should be removed or set right. The living space of the individual should be properly lit up. Night lamps should be provided in corridors and bedrooms if the person must move at night. Flashlights should be handy at the bedside. The bedside lamp should be easily accessible. When getting up at night to use the restroom, the elderly person should be advised to stand for a couple of minutes before moving.

- Whenever needed, assistive devices like walking sticks, handrails, walkers or grab bars in the toilets should be provided to prevent falls and injury. Rubber mats should be provided in the showers and tubs. As far as possible, throw rugs should be removed and carpet edges should be fixed and secured to prevent tripping and falling. Clutter in the room should be avoided. Loose cords and wires littering the floor should be removed. (*See section on 'Stroke'*)
- Changes may be made outdoor in the homes to help the elderly and prevent falls. Cracked sidewalks should be properly repaired and handrails provided in steps. Whenever possible, steps should be replaced with ramps. The elderly person should be encouraged to use a walking-assist device like a walker or walking stick while moving outdoors.
- Any visual disturbances in the patient should be corrected. *Cataracts* should be diagnosed early and operated when needed. An annual eye check-up should be mandated. Bifocal lenses pose a hazard while climbing down steps. The elderly should be warned of this.

Being wary of falls and making the home elderly-friendly goes a long way in preventing such tripping hazards in the elderly.

Resources

1. Davidson's Principles and Practice of Medicine. 23rd Ed. Elsevier. 2018. Chapter 25. Neurology. Pages. 1061-1146
2. Subtle neurological abnormalities as risk factors for cognitive and functional decline, cerebrovascular events, and mortality in older community-dwelling adults. Inzitari M, Pozzi C, Ferrucci L et al. Arch Intern Med 2008;168:1270–6.)
3. Memory, Forgetfulness and Aging: What's normal and what's not – National Institute on Aging.
4. Elderly Stroke Rehabilitation: Overcoming the Complications and Its Associated Challenges: Lui SK and Nguyen MH. Current Gerontology & Geriatrics Research. 2018.

5. Stroke in the Very Old: A Systematic Review of Studies on Incidence, Outcome, and Resource Use: Russo T et al, J. of Aging Research 2011 Aug.

6. The Truth About Aging and Dementia. Alzheimer's Disease and Healthy Aging.

Centres for Diseases Control and
Prevention.

7 Caring for an Older Adult? How to Detect
Delirium in your Loved One, and What
You Can Do. Society of Behavioural
Medicine. Derry H, Shaw A:

Chapter 3. LUNGS - RESPIRATORY SYSTEM

*Structure & Function. The lungs are two
pink, spongy cone-shaped organs located in the
chest cavity on either side of the heart. Together
they weigh about 1.3 kg (2.9 lbs) The right lung is
divided into three segments called **Lobes** and the
left lung into two lobes. Air enters the lungs through
our nose (or mouth), throat, voice box (**Larynx**)
and the windpipe (**Trachea**), The trachea divides
into smaller branches called **Bronchi** which further
branch to end in tiny balloon-like air spaces in the
lungs called **Alveoli**. The lungs are the main
organs in the Respiratory system which
supplement the heart and circulatory system to
make oxygen available to all the organs in the
body.* **(See Fig. 3 & 4)**

The lungs contain around 2400 km (1500 miles) of airways and about 300-500 million air spaces or alveoli.

The function of breathing is automatic and is controlled by the nervous system. Normally we breath 12-20 times a minute. But we can control breathing voluntarily also. When we inhale we draw in air into the lungs. This oxygen in air diffuses into the blood which is brought to the lungs by the pulmonary artery and its branches. At the same time, carbon dioxide from blood is released into the air in the air spaces of the lung. This air is then expelled when we breath out. This exchange of oxygen and carbon dioxide is the main function of the lung.

The oxygen-rich blood from the lungs is carried to the left atrium of the heart through four pulmonary veins, two from each lung. From the left atrium, the blood enters the left ventricle and then to the aorta to be distributed to all parts of the body.

*The lungs are kept clean as far as possible by natural processes in the body. Large particles in the air we breathe are prevented from entering the nose by hairs which are present at the entrance of the nostrils. Inside the walls of the nose, throat, larynx, and bronchi there are fine microscopic hair-like structures called **Cilia** which trap any other tiny particles that may be present in the air that we inhale. These are caught by the cilia and swept outside towards the throat. The cells in the lung also produce a sticky substance called **Mucus** which traps these particles and wafts them towards the throat to be spat out or swallowed. This mucus is secreted in large amounts when we have an infection like a common cold and this causes the copious nasal discharge and sputum which we cough and spit out. Thus, the lungs tend to clean themselves.*

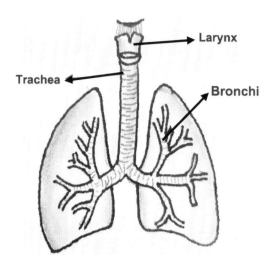

Figure 3

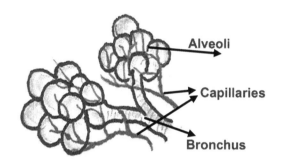

Figure 4

Aging is a complex biological process. Plenty of irreversible changes occur in the organs of the body and their function. The lungs are also not spared. The Respiratory system comprises all the organs that are involved in breathing namely, the nose, throat, larynx, trachea, bronchi, and the lungs. The respiratory system undergoes changes in its anatomical structure, function, and immunological status with aging. Changes in the lungs occurring with age increase its susceptibility to disease. Respiratory disorders are common in old age. Unfortunately, they are underdiagnosed and undertreated in many elderly individuals. Any respiratory disease is more dangerous and perhaps fatal in old age. It has been reported that *one in seven* adults over middle age have one or other respiratory problems.

There are many changes that occur in the lungs with aging. The air spaces enlarge in size thereby leading to a decrease in the surface area available for exchange of oxygen and carbon dioxide. Furthermore, the ability to diffuse oxygen and carbon dioxide by the lung is also decreased in old age. The chest wall muscles which aid in breathing are also comparatively weaker in the elderly and this affects breathing and coughing. Normally there are fine hair like structures which line the whole respiratory tract, called *cilia* which help to sweep the secretions in the lungs towards to mouth to be expelled by coughing and spitting. This clearing action of the cilia is also impaired in old age thereby decreasing the ability to get rid of mucus from the lungs and airways. The force with which one is able to cough is also reduced. The elastic nature of the lungs also is defective and all these put together lead to difficulty in breathing and breathlessness.

Nearly 15% of older adults in the US suffer from respiratory problems reports the **CDC**. Seventeen percent of people between the ages of 60 and 79 had asthma whereas it was only 14% in the 40-59 age group. Air pollution, occupational diseases of the lung and smoking contribute to a large extent the health of the lung in the middle aged and the elderly.

The most common symptoms in the elderly encountered with the problems of lungs are breathlessness, decrease in exercise tolerance and cough. Cough is a common symptom seen in about one-fourth of the elderly. Similarly, breathlessness on exertion is noticeable in about 30% of the elderly over the age of 65. In the elderly these two symptoms should not be ignored and the cause should be investigated and treated. It should be noted that breathlessness could be due to causes other than lung diseases, like heart disease, diseases of the blood like anemia and many other illnesses.

The common respiratory diseases which trouble the elderly are Asthma, Chronic Obstructive Pulmonary Disease (COPD) and Lung Cancer. There are many other diseases which are not very common like Interstitial fibrosis, Pulmonary hypertension etc. In many developing countries, Tuberculosis (TB) of the lung is still a major problem.

CHRONIC OBSTRUCTIVE PULMONARY DISEASE

Chronic Obstructive Pulmonary Disease **(COPD)** is a chronic progressive disease of the lung where long term obstruction occurs to the flow of air in the lung. The airways become narrow making it difficult to breathe. COPD affects about 16 million Americans. It is a public health problem all over the world. COPD is three times more common in persons over the age of 60.

Smoking is the major cause of COPD. But repeated exposure to smoke indoors as in cooking, dust and industrial fumes can also lead to COPD. Other co-morbidities like osteoporosis or thinning of bones, , anxiety, depression, malnutrition, heart disease and skeletal muscle weakness may accompany the disease in the elderly. About 40 – 70% of patients have associated problems with memory loss or dementia. Approximately 40% are depressed. These changes are attributed to the decrease in the oxygen in the blood and increase in carbon dioxide which in turn affect the metabolism of the brain.

In old age, the chest cavity decreases in size limiting the volume of the lungs. The bones become thinner and the shape and size of the rib cage are thus altered, reducing its capacity to expand when we breathe in. The weakness of the muscles of the chest wall also contributes to increasing the severity of the disease.

What are the causes of COPD

There are various causes as listed below.

- Smoking is the most common and preventable cause of COPD. About 4000 harmful chemicals are present in cigarette smoke and around 40 of them can cause cancer. 60% of COPD are causes by smoking alone. It is important to note that passive smoking also leads to COPD.
- Occupational hazards like exposure to metal and coal dust in mines, asbestos, silica exposure in glass and ceramic industries, cotton and dust from grains can all lead to COPD.
- Exposure to smoke at home or outside as occurs during burning of firewood during winter, air pollution, smog and dust, and fumes from household chemicals are other known causes.
- Repeated lung infections can lead to COPD in later life.
- Increasing age and male gender also increase the chances of COPD.

- There are some rare genetic disorders where COPD is common.

What are the symptoms of COPD

Chronic cough is the commonest symptom. It is more in the mornings when the patient wakes up and he coughs up small quantities of whitish sputum. The cough may decrease as the day advances.

Breathlessness on any activity and the inability to do activities with ease is the next common symptom. The patient finds that even minor activities that he was able to do easily before like climbing a flight of stairs or carrying a shopping bag produce shortness of breath.

Sputum production is more in the morning than the rest of the day. But throughout the day the patient coughs up small quantities of whitish sputum frequently. He feels the need to clear his throat frequently.

Wheezing is an important symptom and is due to the sound produced when air flows under pressure through the narrowed airways in the lungs.

Lack of energy and Fatigue with a tendency to curl up in bed are common symptoms seen in these patients.

Occasionally fever may be noticed if they develop infections with viruses or bacteria. The sputum may become yellow in color or stained with blood during the infections.

COPD may be associated with sleep disorders and muscle pain. Chest pain, though not a common symptom, may occur due to the strain on the muscles that help breathing.

When COPD leads to heart failure in later stages, swelling of the feet or ankles may be seen in the patients. This is an alarming symptom needing immediate medical attention.

Patients with COPD need immediate medical attention if they develop sudden and extreme breathlessness. This may be due to an infection or may portend a more serious illness like sudden rupture of a small, ballooned area of lung (*bullae*) leading to air escaping outside the lung and compressing it (**Pneumothorax**). This is a medical emergency. High fever, blood in the sputum are all indications for emergency medical care.

The treatment of the disease is more palliative than curative. The aim of treatment is to improve the quality of life of the patient. The physician often prescribes inhalers with steroids, tablets to increase the airway size and resorts to other measures like *nebulization* when needed. The cause of the disease like smoke in the home, dust etc., are to be identified and avoided. During exacerbations of the disease, antibiotics may be needed. The patient needs to be hospitalized and oxygen supplementation given. The physician will advise the patient to be vaccinated against influenza, pneumonia and Covid. Rarely, surgery may be needed in certain patients.

Rehabilitation in COPD.

The patient is rehabilitated through education regarding the disease and how to take care of himself. The person is encouraged mild physical exercises to the limit of his capacity. Simple exercises like walking, stationary bicycles, climbing stairs or mild weight lifting are suggested.

Adequate nutrition is provided and the patient is encouraged to eat frequent small meals as he may not tolerate single large meals.

Breathing exercises are an important part of rehabilitation. There are various types of breathing exercises which the patient is trained to do. Some of these exercises are as follows:

- Pursed lip breathing: Inhale, purse lips as if whistling or blowing out candles, then breath out.
- Coordinated breathing: Inhale through the nose, purse lips and breathe out during exercises like biceps exercise, bending,

abdominal exercises or simple arm exercises.

- Deep Breathing: Sit with back erect. Take a deep breath, hold for five seconds, and then breathe out. This is called *Pranayama* in the yoga exercises.
- Diaphragmatic Breathing: May be done sitting up or lying down. One hand is placed on the chest and the other over the abdomen. Take a deep breath and feel the abdomen move out. Breathe out pursing the lips.
- Playing the harmonica, blowing into a balloon multiple times or into a football bladder are also simple exercises for the lung. There are also simple plastic devices which can be used to provide breathing exercises to the patient.

These exercises may be taught to the patient by a physical therapist and can be done at home regularly two or three times a day.

Prevention of COPD

Prevention of COPD is more important than its treatment as the disease is not totally curable. Prevention starts in the younger individuals. However, elderly people with propensity to develop COPD should take extra precautions.

- Avoiding smoking is the most important preventive measure. Individuals should also take care to avoid passive smoke exposure in clubs, restaurants, and other closed environments. Government mandate in prevention of smoking in public areas goes a long way in curbing the incidence of the disease.

- Regular exercise is needed to keep the lung functioning optimally in young age. As the person grows older, the exercises should be continued and adjusted to suit the person's stamina.

- Avoiding pollution at home and outside is of paramount importance. Avoid smoking indoors. Also avoid smoke in the home like incense smoke and cooking with firewood as is done in some countries even now. Using detergents and cleaning agents which are less toxic, and using a face mask, preferably the N-95 mask while doing the dusting and cleaning at home are some of the precautions that one should take. Wet wiping of windows or wet-mopping or vacuuming floors should be preferred to dusting, sweeping, or shaking out rugs and carpets. Indoor air freshener and other aerosol sprays should be avoided. Also, fireplaces in homes are better avoided.

- Avoid exposure to air pollution. Burning waste and other materials in the garden is not to be done. A facemask should be worn if one has respiratory problems or if there is a heavy smog.

- <u>Keeping away from patients</u> who have respiratory infections, even a common cold is important.
- <u>Frequent hand washing</u> helps to prevent infections.
- <u>Vaccination</u> for Influenza, Covid and Pneumonia should be taken by the patients.

How to stop smoking

A few tips on how to stop smoking will be in order in a discussion on COPD. The following tips may help a person give up the smoking habit. But the most important fact is to have a strong will power to stop the habit.

- Decide to quit today. Don't decide to do it next week or next month.
- Remove all cigarettes from the home, car, or office.
- Exercise regularly and eat nutritious food. Drink plenty of fluids. Try simple exercises for five minutes when there is a craving for a cigarette.
- To overcome cravings, seek the help of your physician to get you nicotine gum or patches if absolutely necessary.
- Do not mingle with smoker friends. Keep company with friends who do not smoke.
- Get help from groups which are there to help overcome the habit.

- The most important is not to give up trying to quit but being persistent with a strong will.

Understanding the logistics of smoking will be in order at this juncture. On an average, a pack of cigarettes in the US costs $6.65. If a person smokes one pack of cigarettes a day, the person will be spending $2427.25 per year. This works out to a very large amount over a period of ten or twenty years. The money saved by relinquishing smoking hence is enormous.

ASTHMA

Unlike COPD, Asthma is a recurrent and reversible disease of the respiratory system and is due to intermittently occurring narrowing of the airways. Approximately, 4 - 13% of elderly people in the US over the age of 65 have asthma. They are five times more likely to die from asthma. This type of 'late onset asthma' is more in women. In the elderly, asthma may be more serious than in the young and may be deadly. The mortality is higher, the acute attacks of asthma last for longer periods often necessitating longer hospital stays. Asthma is often confused with COPD.

Why is asthma more serious in the elderly?

The burden of co-existing conditions like heart disease, diabetes, high blood pressure, are more in the elderly. Often asthma is underdiagnosed in the elderly. The asthma related symptoms may not be properly diagnosed. In some individuals, asthma starts early in life and then remits for a long period only to reappear again in old age. In the elderly the asthma may be intermittent or persistent when it becomes more difficult to manage.

What triggers asthma attacks?

Attacks of asthma can be triggered commonly by dust, pollen, animal dander, allergens, air pollution, inhaled chemicals, and smoke. A bout of common cold can often trigger an asthmatic attack. Obese individuals, smokers, those with chronic sinusitis and the elderly with snoring problems during sleep are prone to develop asthma. Other problems like nasal allergy and *Gastroesophageal reflux*, which denotes the food contents from the stomach flowing back into the food pipe causing a burning sensation in the chest, may also induce asthma. In some individuals a bout of exercise can induce asthmatic attacks. Certain medications used in heart diseases like Beta-blockers can induce asthma in susceptible individuals. Other medications like aspirin and other pain killers also may trigger asthma.

The main symptoms of asthma are wheezing, cough, chest tightness and breathlessness. The sputum produced is watery and scanty. The cough is often more.

Treatment of Asthma. The main treatment is the use of inhalers of *steroids* which the physician prescribes. In addition, occasionally steroids may be given as tablets. Other medications are also given which increase the size of the airways and relieve the narrowing.

Acute infections when present are appropriately treated with antibiotics. Oxygen support and hospitalization will be needed in some cases of acute attacks of asthma.

In some patients, the use of nebulizers at home may be needed for the treatment of asthmatic attacks.

Prevention of Asthma

The following points should be remembered in preventing asthmatic attacks. (*Also see section on COPD*).

- Exposure to cold dry air should be avoided.
- Abrupt changes in weather should be avoided as far as possible.
- Allergens like pet dander, dust, and pollen can worsen asthma. Mattresses and pillows may be covered with special allergy proof

covers. Carpets may have to be removed if they collect dust. Heavy curtains may be avoided in homes. Vacuuming should be preferred to dusting and damp wiping of surfaces to remove dust should be practiced at home.

- Strong odors and fumes from chemicals, irritants, bleach, room fresheners, paint and perfumes should be avoided. The use of incense in the house may induce attacks of asthma. Aerosols may be avoided as far as possible.

- Pets must be kept out of bedrooms and areas with carpets or furniture with cloth upholstery to avoid pet dander. If pets are the cause for the asthma, it is wise not to have them.

- Smoke and smog should be averted. Masks (N-95) should be worn outdoors if there is air pollution. Indoor masks should be worn during cleaning, dusting etc. Don't permit anyone to smoke in your home or in your car.

- Detect the triggers in individual patients like medications, exercise etc., and try to avert them.

- Air conditioners and heating filters must be kept dry. Use exhaust fans in toilets, kitchen and other areas when needed.

- Carry your medications and prescriptions with you whenever you travel.

- Regular breathing exercises are helpful in preventing asthma in most patients.

LUNG CANCER

Worldwide, the population is shifting towards older ages as their numbers increase. This shift increases the risk of developing various cancers of which lung cancer is an important one. Lung cancer is one of the leading causes of cancer related deaths. The peak incidence of lung cancer is in the age group of 60 – 75 years.

In the US, 68% of lung cancer patients are diagnosed after the age of 65 and 14% after the age of 80. 90% of lung cancers are seen in those above the age of 55. The disease is more in males. The treatment options also vary depending on the age of the patient. Unlike the young, surgery may not be the best option for an elderly patient. In advanced cases of lung cancer, the approximate survival is for one year only.

Symptoms of lung cancer are mainly cough, not getting cured or worsening, coughing out blood, hoarseness of the voice, shortness of breath, unexplained weight loss, loss of appetite, excessive fatigue, and repeated infections like pneumonia, bronchitis or wheezing occurring for the first time in an elderly patient. Occasionally the diseases does not produce symptoms till it spreads to other areas of the body and is far advanced.

Lung cancer spreads to other areas of the body as it grows in size. Spread to the bones produces pain in the back, hips, and other bones of the body. Dissemination to the brain may present with headaches, weakness of the arms or legs, epileptic fits, giddiness etc. Extension to the liver produces jaundice which is seen as yellow coloring of the eyeball. In the lymph nodes, it may be seen as swelling of these nodes in various parts of the body like the neck, axilla, and groin.

What are the Risk Factors that cause Lung Cancer

Various risk factors and causes have been identified in the causation of lung cancer.

- Tobacco smoke stands out as the number one cause culprit in causing lung cancer. Other tobacco products like snuff, pipe smoking and cigars also lead to lung cancer. Smoking cannabis also causes it. It has to be emphasized that second hand smoke is equally important in causing lung cancer. It has been reported that 80% of lung cancer deaths are related to smoking.

- Exposure to Radon which is a radioactive gas has been identified as another risk factor. Radon is present in soil and rocks in some areas and results from the breakdown of uranium, a radioactive substance. Radon is an odorless and tasteless gas which may be found in higher concentration in houses indoors or in water taken from underground sources like wells. Chronic exposure to this indoors may be causative of lung cancer. Miners who work deep underground also may be exposed to the gas.
- Asbestos is another product which is highly *carcinogenic* (meaning, causing cancer). It may be present in mines, mills, and asbestos insulations. Inhalation of asbestos over time leads to a lung condition called *Asbestosis* which ultimately may lead to lung cancer.
- Inhalation of chemicals like Arsenic, Cadmium, Beryllium, Silica, Nickel, and diesel exhaust fumes may also cause lung cancer.
- Previous radiation treatment to the lungs for breast cancer and other diseases can lead to cancer.
- Air pollution has been reported to be a cause of cancer of the lung.
- Persons with a family history of lung cancer are also more likely to develop the disease.

- <u>Tuberculosis and other lung diseases</u> which cause scarring of the lung also lead to lung cancer in some patients. Infection with HIV virus (AIDS) is a risk factor in the development of lung cancer.

The treatment options for Lung cancer are many. Treatment is planned by a team of specialist physicians which includes the *Pulmonologist* and the *Oncologist* (Chest diseases and Cancer specialists respectively). In the elderly, the treatment may be different from that in the younger patient.

The options available are Surgery during the early stages when the tumor can be easily removed. Chemotherapy, Radiation therapy, and Immunotherapy are the other modes of treatment. In immunotherapy medications are used which stimulate the patient's immune system to attack and kill the cancer cells. Newer modes of treatment are also being developed and research is ongoing in this field. When the cancer has spread to other areas of the body, it is often Palliative Treatment that is needed.

Can Lung Cancer be prevented

The importance of preventing lung cancer cannot be overemphasized.

- Avoidance of smoking is of paramount importance in preventing lung cancer. This campaign should be started among the younger generation in schools and colleges. The government should take strong measures to discourage smoking which often starts in teenage due to peer pressure. Using tobacco in any form must be avoided.

- Exposure to the cancer-causing agents as has been described previously should be limited by use of adequate personal protective devices by the individual, especially those in occupations where the chances of exposure are high.
- Radon exposure in houses can be assessed by appropriate testing agencies and measures taken to reduce the exposure.
- A healthy diet and lifestyle go a long way in preventing the disease.
- Cancer screening programs are available and done by the government in various countries and this facility must be availed of by the elderly, especially those who are at a risk.

Lung cancer, thus, is a disease which has to be prevented and the treatment though effective in the majority, may not be very successful in the elderly due to various causes. In the elderly only palliative care is possible at later stages of the disease.

OTHER LUNG DISEASES

Various other lung diseases also cause problems for the elderly. Infections of various types are not uncommon. One such infection is Tuberculosis (TB). This is an infection which affects the lung and is a common disease in many parts of the world. It is a infectious disease and is caused by the Tuberculosis bacteria. The commonest mode of spread is through aerosol particles released when a diseased person coughs. The disease is now curable with long term use of antibiotics.

In the elderly, the disease is often a reactivation of a tuberculosis infection that was acquired in younger age. The disease presents with cough, fever, spitting of blood and progressive loss of weight. In the elderly individuals, the disease may be more severe especially as their immunity is low. Diagnosis is by X ray examination of the chest and examining the sputum for the TB bacteria.

Various drugs are used in the treatment of TB and often a combination of medications is used in the treatment. The treatment is for long periods as the bacteria are often resistant to ordinary antibiotics and special drugs are needed for the treatment.

In addition, there are many other occupational lung diseases that may plague the elderly and render them miserable in old age.

Resources.

1. Davidson's Principles and Practice of Medicine. 23rd. Ed. Elsevier 2018. Chapter 17- Respiratory Medicine, pages 545-628.

2. Respiratory & breathing issues in the elderly 2021. West Hartford Health & Rehabilitation Center

3. The Aging Lung : Lowery EM et al. Clinical Interventions in Aging. 2013. 8 : 1489 – 1496.

4.COPD in the Elderly. The Aging Lung. Jayadev A, Gill SK. Geriatric Medicine Journal. Oct. 2017

5.Lung Cancer in Elderly Patients . Venuta F, Diso D, Onorati I et al. J. of Thoracic diseases. 2016. No 8 Suppl 11 (5908-5914

6.Master the Art of Aging Gracefully by Vikram Khaitan (Amazon.com)

Chapter 4. KIDNEYS & BLADDER – THE URINARY SYSTEM

Structure & Function. The kidneys are two reddish-brown bean shaped organs which are present on both sides of the spine in the lower part of our abdomen at the back. Each kidney is about 12 cms (4 ½ inches) long. Each weighs about 80 – 160 gms (3-6 oz). Each kidney is attached to long muscular tubes through a funnel shaped structure at its concave border called the **Renal Pelvis.** (Renal = adjective of Kidney). These long tubes are called **Ureters**, which carry the urine produced in the kidneys to the **Urinary Bladder** which is situated in the lower abdomen. **(See Fig.5)** The urinary bladder collects and stores the urine produced by the kidneys which is then passed out when the person feels the sensation to urinate. The kidneys are supplied by two arteries which carry blood to the kidney. They are called **Renal Arteries.** Similarly, the **Renal Veins** carry the blood away from the kidney.

The functional unit of the kidney is a microscopic structure called the **Nephron.** The nephron is the 'filtering unit' of the kidney. Each kidney has 1 million such nephrons. The filtering part of the Nephron is shaped like a wine-cup and is called the **Bowman's capsule.** The tiny blood vessels (capillaries) enter these 'cups' and form a small cauliflower-like bunch. This is called the

Glomerulus. **(See Fig. 6)** *The waste materials in the blood seep out of the capillaries into the Bowman's capsule which is connected to long, minute tubes called* **Renal Tubules**. *These convey the filtered waste products along with water. The tubules join together to form larger tubules which then carry this urine into the funnel shaped structure at the concave margin of the kidney- the renal pelvis. The renal pelvis is connected to the ureter which conveys the urine into the bladder.*

The kidney receives one-fourth to one-fifth of the total blood pumped by the heart. It functions like a wastewater treatment plant helping to rid the body of the waste products of metabolism. The amount of fluid filtered by the two kidneys per day is about 180 liters (48 gallons). But all this is not excreted as urine. 99% of the water in this filtrate is re-absorbed by the kidney along with some essential electrolytes like sodium, magnesium, calcium, and potassium. Glucose and **amino acids** *are also reabsorbed. Majority of the water filtered is reabsorbed so that the urine becomes more and more concentrated as it passes along these tiny tubules.*

An average person with a normal fluid intake produces around 800 – 2000 ml (30-60 oz) of urine per day.

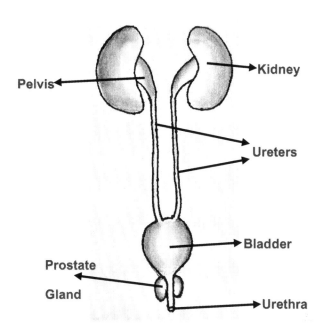

Figure 5 (Kidneys-Bladder)

The **Urinary Bladder**, which is a muscular bag, located in the front part of the lower abdomen protected by bone, stores the urine, and at regular intervals the urine is passed when the patient feels the sensation.

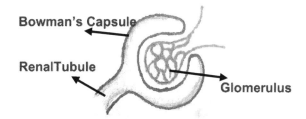

Figure 6. (Glomerulus)

Many changes occur in the kidneys and the urinary bladder with age. The filtering units of the kidneys are microscopic structures called '***Nephrons***'. Their number decreases with age. The kidney also tends to become smaller in size with age. The functional capacity of the kidneys decrease and they are able to filter the waste products from the blood only at a slower rate. The blood vessels supplying the kidneys also become thickened and may become narrow, decreasing the blood supply to the kidneys thereby further affecting their working.

The wall of the urinary bladder becomes less elastic and stiffer as age advances. Thereby the bladder cannot stretch to accommodate more urine, hence the bladder becomes full quickly and cannot hold as much urine as before. The muscles of the bladder also weaken with age. In men the urethra which is the tubular structure which conveys urine from the bladder externally, becomes narrow because the prostate gland through which the urethra passes enlarges compressing the urethra.

Chronic Kidney failure, urinary infections and urinary incontinence which is the inability to hold urine are the most common problems in old age.

CHRONIC KIDNEY DISEASE

The filtering function of the kidneys remain normal till the fourth decade of life. Thereafter there is a gradual reduction in the function over years and is accelerated after the age of 60. The weight of the kidney also starts decreasing after the age of 50.

Chronic Kidney disease (CKD) kills more people annually than breast or prostate cancer. Roughly, 50% of those above the age of 75 have kidney disease. Whereas the prevalence of CKD in the normal adult population of the US is about 11%, in the elderly over the age of 60, it is approximately 40%.

What are the Risk Factors causing CKD

The diseases which accelerate age related chronic kidney disease are as follows:

- High Blood Pressure or Hypertension
- Diabetes mellitus
- High levels of fat in blood especially cholesterol
- Smoking
- Overweight and Obesity
- Male gender
- Lead exposure
- Atherosclerotic disease

- Previous history of Acute diseases of kidney.
- Heart failure due to any cause.
- Medications and Toxins. There are many medications that can lead to CKD if used for long periods. The commonest being pain killers. Excessive and irrational use of pain killers is dangerous. Some toxic herbs prescribed by certain healers can cause CKD. Exposure to heavy metals also can lead to CKD.
- Diseases of the kidney like repeated Urinary infections, Kidney stones and cancer of the bladder or prostate can lead to CKD.

What are the symptoms of CKD

Often CKD is diagnosed when a routine blood examination is done for Serum Creatinine and Blood Urea. These are two products of metabolism in the body which are normally cleared by the kidney and the blood levels of these substances are kept reasonably low. But when the kidney begins to fail, the blood level of these two chemicals increases and is detectable by a simple test.

Many symptoms may not occur during the early stages even when the blood level of creatinine and urea are high. The first symptom usually is increase in urination occurring at night. The patient needs to get up many times at night to pass urine. Later on, tiredness, and breathlessness may appear. The tiredness is often due to the anemia which these patients develop. Weight loss, nausea, and vomiting, muscle cramps, itching all over the body, weight loss and loss of appetite occur. The patient looks pale and there is often swelling in the lower limbs due to fluid overload in the body.

The doctor will order investigations for the patient. Laboratory examination of the urine shows protein in the urine. The patient may often complain that his urine froths on passing into the toilet bowl. Appropriate blood investigations and other tests reveal the disease. The blood shows high levels of creatinine and blood urea.

How is CKD treated

The treatment of CKD is mainly to treat the underlying cause of the CKD. Diabetes and High Blood Pressure, if present, must be well controlled. Urinary infections should be treated with antibiotics. Surgery may be needed if there is an enlarged prostate causing the CKD. Other causes should be addressed appropriately. These measures to a large extent reduce the progression of the disease and make it slower. Medications are prescribed to treat the anemia which occurs in CKD.

The diet of the patient needs special care. A dietician will be able to provide an appropriate diet for the patient. As CKD can increase the blood levels of Potassium, extra care should be taken to avoid foods rich in potassium. Some of these foods with high levels of potassium are given below.

- Fruits like bananas, avocados, figs.
- Vegetables like Tomatoes, sprouts, spinach, potatoes, parsnips. When vegetables are boiled the potassium content decreases.
- Sweets and snacks like chocolate, toffee, nuts
- Fruit juices, milk, yoghurt, coconut water, beer
- Salt substitutes like Lo-Salt.

In patients who still continue to have high levels of creatinine and blood urea, the physician will advise dialysis to get rid of the accumulated waste products from the blood and the excess water in the body.

The consideration for a renal transplantation in old age is a matter of discussion and many factors have to be taken into consideration before the decision to offer renal transplantation to an elderly patient is decided. Often the post-transplantation treatment with medications is not tolerated by the elderly patient and hence a conservative approach with a chronic dialysis program may have to be adopted.

What complications can occur in CKD

Chronic Kidney Disease can cause certain metabolic complications in the patient. They are described below.

1. **Gout**. Gout is a condition where the blood levels of a chemical - Uric Acid increase. Uric acid is a chemical produced when some food products are broken down in the body. CKD can cause gout. Gout also can occur as an independent disease and cause kidney disease. The disease affects the joints and produces severe painful arthritis.

2. **Anemia**. It is an almost inevitable complication of CKD and must be treated with medications and occasionally blood transfusion. When CKD occurs, the body cannot produce enough red blood cells. This leads to anemia. The anemia causes excess fatigue in the patient and as the blood cannot carry enough oxygen, the patient feels breathless with even minor effort.

3. **Metabolic Acidosis**. This is due to the increased buildup of acids in the body. Acidosis can lead to bone loss –

osteoporosis which makes the person prone to fractures.

4. Blood levels of **Phosphorus** can increase causing bone disease leading to weakening of bones, muscle cramps and bone and joint pain.

5. **Heart disease** can occur as a complication of CKD, which may be the cause of death in these individuals.

6. **High Blood Potassium.** Blood levels of potassium may increase leading to symptoms of severe weakness, and muscle cramps. But the most dangerous effect of high potassium is that it may trigger abnormal rhythm of the heart (*Arrhythmia*) which may prove fatal if not promptly treated.

7. **Swelling in the body**. Increase in fluid buildup in the body can lead to swelling in the legs, face, and abdomen. Normally the excess fluid in the body is filtered and removed by the kidneys as urine. In CKD, this is impaired and hence fluid accumulates in the body. It is seen as swelling of the legs and ankles, puffiness of the face especially around the eyes, breathlessness. Inability to lie down flat due to breathlessness is caused by fluid in the lungs. This is controlled by reducing the intake of liquids as per the advice of the doctor and removing the excess body fluid by dialysis.

URINARY INFECTION

Urinary Tract Infections (**UTI**) in the elderly are common and can affect the Kidneys, Ureters, Bladder, or the Urethra. It is more common in females and causes more morbidity and mortality compared to the younger patient with UTI. Usually, it starts below in the urethra and creeps up the bladder and the ureters to the kidneys. When the infection spreads to the blood, it can be deadly. The symptoms also may be variable in the elderly unlike in the young.

Why are the elderly prone to UTI

About 10% of women over the age of 65 have UTI each year. It may increase to 30% in those above 80. There are many reasons for this.

- The elderly individual has a poor immune status and is prone for all types of infections.
- Estrogen, the female hormone in women has a rather protective effect on UTI. But after menopause and in old age this protection is lost.

- In women, the urethral opening and the vaginal opening are close together. Hence, bacteria can easily get into the urethra from the vagina. The muscles of the pelvis also weaken during old age and render the women more prone to UTI.
- The elderly males and females often find it difficult to empty the bladder fully when passing urine and some amount of urine remains in the bladder. In men, an enlarged prostate may aggravate this. Also, narrowing of the urethra or ureters called '*stricture*' can cause difficulty in passing urine leading to UTI. This residual urine which stagnates in the bladder tends to breed harmful bacteria which cause UTI.
- Often the elderly may not take care of themselves and may not be able to maintain proper genital hygiene. This may be more so in patients with cognitive impairment.
- Other associated conditions like prolapse of the uterus may co-exist in females and this may increase the chances of UTI.
- Co-morbidities like Diabetes increase the chances of UTI especially as their urine contains high levels of glucose which contributes to the multiplication of bacteria. The presence of stones in the kidneys or bladder increases the chances of UTI.

- The elderly are less communicative and tend to underplay their symptoms or ignore them till the infection becomes severe.
- Elderly individuals may have a catheter introduced into the bladder to drain urine as in bedridden patients, those with paralysis, or stroke. This increases the risk of UTI.
- Radiation or surgery to the pelvic region also may lead to UTI.

What are the symptoms of UTI in the elderly

UTI can present with all the symptoms which are seen in the younger persons. Occasionally, certain symptoms in the elderly are atypical and may not indicate that the person is suffering from a UTI. Hence the diagnosis may be missed. The main symptoms seen are as follows:

- A change in the frequency of passing urine may be noticed. The patient has to pass urine very frequently especially at night. In addition, the patient may have the urge to pass urine immediately. If not, they may soil their clothes.
- Pain while passing urine is often a symptom of UTI. The patient feels a severe pain in the urethra or a burning sensation while urinating. A feeling of pressure in the lower abdomen may be felt by some. Even

though there may be an urge to pass urine, only a small amount of urine is passed each time.

- Occasionally, when the infection spreads upwards to the kidney, the patient may feel pain in the lower back or the lower part of the abdomen.
- Passing blood in urine may be seen occasionally and is a frightening symptom. The urine may be cloudy and foul smelling.
- Fever and chills accompany UTI when the infection has affected the bladder or the kidneys.
- Fatigue, nausea, vomiting are other symptoms seen in some elderly patients.
- Some patients may present with confusion which may mislead the relatives or the doctor. This is often seen in those with mild cognitive impairment.
- If the infection is not treated in time, the infection can spread into the kidneys and from there enter the blood to cause a condition named '*sepsis*' where bacteria are present in the blood and travel to other organs of the body. This can be a very serious condition presenting with high fever, shivering, and a fall of blood pressure and it may be fatal.

How is UTI treated.

The mainstay of treatment is the use of antibiotics. First the doctor diagnoses the condition after examining the urine and sending it for culture to identify the bacteria which is causing the infection. The doctor may also order some tests to assess the bladder and its function.

An appropriate antibiotic is then prescribed. Mild infections can be treated with oral antibiotics, but severe infections may need injections of antibiotics. Along with this the patient is encouraged to drink plenty of fluids. Certain medications are prescribed to keep the urine alkaline to hasten recovery. The pain felt by the patient is relieved with certain specific medications which control the pain in the urinary tract.

Any specific causes that leads to repeated UTI like a prostate enlargement, kidney or bladder stones, stricture of the urethra, and prolapse of the uterus, are managed by appropriate surgical measures.

Prevention of UTI in the elderly

Prevention of UTI is of paramount importance especially in those who are unable to take care of themselves. Bedridden patients are more likely to get UTI as some of them may have a catheter introduced into their bladder. Strict hygiene is needed in such cases. For other individuals, the following suggestions would be in order.

- Encourage the person to drink adequate amounts of fluids. Water intake should be encouraged so that the urine is straw-colored and not high colored which indicates a concentrated urine and dehydration.
- Meticulous genital hygiene should be encouraged. The genital area should always be kept clean and dry. Frequent washing of hands must be practiced.
- The elderly individuals should be asked to pass urine more frequently as holding their urine can increase the chances of UTI. Even if they do not have the urge to pass urine, they should be encouraged to do so. A urination schedule should be encouraged and the help of an alarm may be needed in some elderly patients.
- Elderly females may be provided with vaginal creams containing estrogen by their doctor which to some extent prevents them from getting UTI.
- Alcohol, caffeinated drinks, spicy food, citrus juices can irritate the bladder and are better avoided or sparingly consumed.
- The patients should be told to pass urine immediately before and soon after sexual intercourse and wash the genitals.
- Tight clothes should be avoided and loose-fitting cotton underclothes are preferable
- Females should be particularly told to avoid back-to-front wiping after passing stools

and always wiping from front-to-back should be practiced.

- The use of cranberry juice has been advocated in the prevention of UTI as this is said to contain a substance which prevents the sticking of bacteria to the wall of the bladder.

URINARY INCONTINENCE

Aging produces various changes in the kidneys, urinary bladder, ureters, and urethra. The bladder shows changes in its wall. Normally the bladder is an elastic bag which can enlarge in size to accommodate adequate amounts of urine when the person is young. As age advances, the bladder wall becomes stiffer and hence cannot stretch to hold much urine as before. The muscles in the wall of the bladder also weaken. Along with this the muscles in the pelvis also weaken in both males and females, but the problem is more in females as their pelvic muscles may be rendered weak by repeated pregnancies and deliveries. Men may be troubled in addition by an enlargement of the prostate gland.

These changes in the bladder may impair the elderly person's ability to hold urine and this may cause leakage of urine. *Urinary incontinence* is the involuntary passage of urine. The inability to empty the bladder completely is called *'urinary retention'.* The main trouble for the patient is that this symptom of incontinence may affect his or her social life. It may also disrupt his normal work at home or office due to the need to pass urine frequently or soiling of the underclothes. It is seen in 15% of women and 10% of men over 65 years of age.

What are the problems that can affect bladder health

There are some common causes that affect the bladder health of an individual, especially the elderly.

- Constipation causes pressure of the bowels on the bladder thereby disrupting normal function of the bladder.
- Diabetes mellitus is a disease that in later stages affects the nerves in the body and when the nerves to the bladder are affected, bladder control is affected.
- Overweight and obesity can lead to incontinence of urine.
- A person who is more sedentary and does not exercise adequately is more prone for bladder problems.
- Smoking can impair bladder function. It is noticed that bladder cancer is also more in smokers.

- Certain medications like those prescribed for anxiety and depression may 'dull' the nerves of the bladder causing bladder problems.
- Alcohol and caffeinated drinks in excess can worsen bladder problems.
- Some foods and drinks like sodas, artificial sweeteners, spicy foods, citrus fruits, and juices can worsen bladder problems .
- Injury to pelvis which may occur in trauma due to accidents. Childbirth in women who have delivered many children can damage the muscles and nerves that control the bladder.

What are the symptoms of Bladder problems

Many symptoms may presage a bladder problem in the elderly.

- Urinary incontinence which is the inability of the patient to hold urine is often the most common and unpleasant complaint.
- The patient may feel the need to pass urine many times at night.
- A sudden urge to pass urine may be present and unless the person passes urine immediately, he may soil his clothes.
- Pain or a burning sensation may be felt before, during or after passing urine.
- The person may want to pass urine but has trouble starting to urinate. This is seen

more in men who have an enlarged prostate gland.

- The urine stream may be weak and the patient takes a long time to pass urine and empty the bladder.
- Cloudy urine or blood in the urine may be noticed. The urine may be foul smelling in urinary tract infections.

There are various type of incontinence occurring in the elderly. They can be described depending on the symptoms and under what conditions they occur.

1. Stress Incontinence. Normal activities like sneezing, coughing laughing or exerting or lifting a heavy weight can cause the individual to pass urine unconsciously. It is seen almost exclusively in women and is due to weakness of the pelvic muscles.
2. Urge Incontinence. The person feels a sudden and intense urge to pass urine and if he or she does not do so immediately, they are likely to soil their clothes.
3. Overflow Incontinence. This is overflow dribbling of urine from a full bladder without the patient being aware of this.
4. Functional incontinence. This is seen in patients with physical or mental impairment. The person cannot get to the toilet in time or finds it difficult to unbutton his pants or run to the toilet due to diseases like arthritis or muscle weakness.

What are the common causes of Urinary Incontinence.

Urinary incontinence can occur as a symptoms of many diseases of the kidney and the urinary tract and also diseases of the nervous system. Some of the causes of Urinary Incontinence are as follows:

- Urinary Tract infections can cause incontinence as the infections irritates the bladder and causes urgency of urination.
- Long standing constipation with collection of stools in the rectum can put pressure on the bladder and cause incontinence.
- Diseases affecting nerves or damage to nerves as occurs during childbirth or trauma can lead to weakness of the bladder and incontinence. Diabetes can affect the nerves of the bladder and cause incontinence. Stroke in a patient often leads to incontinence.
- Previous surgery on the pelvis, especially in females can weaken the pelvic muscles and lead to incontinence. Males may have incontinence following surgery of the prostate.
- In men an enlarged prostate can lead to difficulty in bladder control and incontinence.

- Delirium in a patient may cause urinary incontinence.
- Excess caffeine or alcohol can cause incontinence since the bladder fills up quickly with urine.
- Certain medications used to treat kidney diseases, high blood pressure and heart failure can cause an excess formation of urine and lead to incontinence.

How is Urinary incontinence treated

The treatment for incontinence is mainly by reducing weight in overweight subjects, prompt treatment of the causes like urinary infections, improving the muscle tone in the pelvic muscles through exercises (*Kegels exercises* – lifting, holding, and then relaxing the pelvic muscles as if to prevent passing urine or gas), Surgical correction of certain abnormalities and usage of a urinary catheter in patients in whom spontaneous voiding is not possible e.g. when they have paralysis of the lower limbs.

Exercises to improve the tone of the pelvic muscles and thigh muscles, avoiding constipation by taking a high fiber diet, controlling one's weight are some of the preventive measures that can be adopted. Other preventive strategies are regular emptying of the bladder, avoiding too much caffeine and alcohol, avoiding lifting heavy weights.

Resources

1. Davidson's Principles and Practice of Medicine. 23rd Edition. Elsevier Publications 2018. Chapter 15. Nephrology and Urology 381-440.
2. Chronic Kidney Disease. NCD Alliance.
3. Chronic Kidney Disease – Articles. The New England Journal of Medicine Articles. 2022
4. Urinary Tract Infections – Review on its Prevalence and Recent Advances. Badiger AS et al. Journal of Pharmaceutical Research International. 33: 582-592. Oct 2021
5. Symptoms of Urinary Tract Infections in Older adults. Health Essentials. Cleveland Clinic.
6. Urinary Incontinence in Older Adults. National Institute on Aging.
7. Urinary Incontinence in Aging. What to know when you can't wait to go. Didyk N. in Better Health While Aging – Leslie Kernisan

Chapter 5. ENDOCRINE SYSTEM

Structure & Function. *The Endocrine System consists of glands in the body which secrete substances called **Hormones** necessary for various metabolic processes in the body. These glands do not have ducts to discharge the hormone, but directly secrete the hormones into the blood stream. Hence they are also called* **'Ductless Glands'**.

The main glands which are part of the endocrine system are the pineal gland, pituitary gland, pancreas, ovaries, testes, thyroid gland, parathyroid glands and the adrenal glands. The part of the brain called the Hypothalamus also is an active member of this group as it regulates the secretion of hormones from all the endocrine glands. The hormones produced by the hypothalamus stimulate the pituitary to secrete its hormones. The hypothalamus also controls the regulation of our body temperature, hunger, sex drive, thirst, salt and water balance, emotions etc. In short, it acts as a co-ordination centre, a smart centre in the brain that helps to maintain the internal state of the body in equilibrium.

The Pituitary gland *is situated in the under surface of the brain from which it hangs by a small stalk. The hormones produced by the pituitary gland under instructions from the hypothalamus*

148

*regulate the release of hormones from the other endocrine glands. (***See Fig. 2. Brain***)*

The Thyroid Gland *is a butterfly-shaped gland which is situated in the front of the neck below the voice box (larynx). It secretes the two Thyroid hormones the release of which in turn is controlled by the hormones released from the pituitary gland.* **(See Fig.7)**

The Parathyroid Glands *are small button-like glands usually four in number situated at the back of the thyroid gland. They secrete the* ***Parathyroid Hormone*** *which regulates Calcium and bone metabolism.*

The Adrenal Glands *are situated like caps at the top of the two kidneys, and they control the immune responses, responses to stress, blood pressure, regulation of water and electrolytes, and other metabolic functions of the body.* <u>*Aldosterone,*</u> <u>*Cortisol*</u> *and* <u>*Adrenaline*</u> *are three important hormones produced by the adrenal gland.* **(See Fig 7)**

The Pancreas *is a gland which secretes pancreatic juice which aids in digestion. It is situated behind the stomach in the upper abdomen. But it contains within it two types of cell clusters which secrete two hormones concerned with the regulation of blood sugar. These are* ***Insulin*** *and* ***Glucagon***. *Insulin helps in*

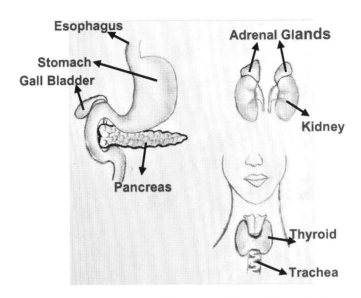

Figure 7 (Endocrine Glands)

keeping the blood sugar normal and helping the cells take up glucose and convert it into energy. Glucagon helps to release glucose from the liver whenever the blood glucose level tends to become low. **(See Fig 7)**

The Testes in the male and the Ovaries in the females also act as endocrine glands and secrete the male and female hormones respectively. The male hormone is Testosterone, and the female hormones are Estrogen and Progesterone which regulate the menstrual cycle of females.

The Pineal Gland is a small structure tucked deep in the brain between the two cerebral hemispheres. (See Fig. 2. Brain) It secretes the hormone Melatonin which is concerned with the regulation of the daily cycle in humans (Circadian Rhythm) and modulates sleep patterns.

In addition to these specific endocrine glands, many of the other organs of the body also have specialized cells which secrete hormones needed for regulating some of their functions. The heart, the kidneys, the fat cells in the body, the skin cells, the cells in the stomach and intestines and the placenta during pregnancy also secrete hormones.

DIABETES MELLITUS

Diabetes mellitus (DM) is a common disease of the elderly population. Our body converts food into glucose which in turn is converted to energy needed for the normal functioning of the body. Insulin is required to convert glucose into energy,. In diabetics, insulin is secreted in smaller amounts or the available insulin is not able to act properly and the body is unable to utilize the insulin that is secreted.

The meaning of the word *'Diabetes'* in Greek means 'passing through' or 'a large discharge of urine'. *'Mellitus'* means 'sweet tasting like honey'.

Diabetes mellitus is of two types. The disease seen usually in children and young adults is called Type 1 Diabetes mellitus. Here the secretion of insulin is markedly reduced and the patient has to be on insulin treatment for life.

Type 2 Diabetes mellitus is seen in adults and the elderly. This is the most common type and starts in middle age.

Pre diabetes is a condition where the blood sugars are higher than normal but do not reach levels sufficient to diagnose the person as diabetic. This is the stage before frank diabetes develops. Majority of these patients in later life turn diabetic unless they undertake rigorous preventive measures.

Long-standing high blood sugars can lead to damage to various organs of the body like the eye, heart, blood vessels, kidneys, and nerves.

How prevalent is the disease

Approximately 37.3 million Americans are said to suffer from DM which is 1 out of 10 persons of the population. One out of five patients do not know that they are diabetic. In persons over the age of 65, the prevalence is 29.2% which adds up to 15.9 million elderly persons. Around 1.4 million new cases of diabetes are diagnosed in the US annually. Prediabetes is seen in 96 million Americans over the age of 18. According to the WHO, DM is the ninth leading cause of death globally.

In 2019 in India, 77 million patients with DM were present which is expected to increase to 134 million by 2045. Approximately half of these individuals remain undiagnosed. The prevalence of DM in India is 11.8%.

What are the symptoms of Diabetes mellitus.

Diabetes can cause serious health problems due to the chronic increase in blood sugar in the individual. The symptoms with which the patient comes to the doctor are often as follows.

- Frequent urination. The increased amount of glucose in the blood causes the kidneys to overwork to get rid of this and when glucose is passed in urine, water accompanies it. Thus, the patient has to pass urine frequently.
- Thirst. The increase in urination tends to dehydrate the patient and he feels intense thirst to compensate for the loss of fluid from the body. The mouth, throat and lips become dry.
- Excessive Hunger. As the body cannot use insulin properly, the patient feels hungrier. There tends to be a predilection for sweet foods particularly.
- Changes in the vision. This is seen in some individuals. The lens in the eye changes shape according to the change in blood

glucose levels and this leads to blurring of vision.

- Frequent infections. Diabetes predisposes to frequent infections like urinary tract infections, respiratory infections, and infections of the skin. Fungal infections may persistently occur in the groin and axilla. Genital infections in men and women are not infrequent.

- Fatigue. Severe fatigue and weakness may be seen in some individuals. They feel tired all the time.

- Weight Loss. Unexplained weight loss is another frequently noted symptom in many.

- Slow healing. Injuries and wounds take longer time to heal in diabetics. Occasionally this may be the first symptoms when the disease gets diagnosed.

- Gum disease. The gums of the mouth may be red and swollen due to infection and occasionally they may contain pockets of pus in them causing the teeth to loosen.

- Nerve disease. When the nerves are affected, a numbness and tingling feeling may be noted in the hands and feet. This is called 'Polyneuropathy'.

- Headache. Some patients feel a persistent headache.

- <u>Mood changes</u>. Irritability, apathy, inability to concentrate or depression may be seen in some individuals.
- <u>Patches of blackened skin</u> may be noticed in the body folds and creases like the armpit, groin or back of the neck. This is called *'Acanthosis Nigricans'*.

What are the Risk Factors to develop Diabetes mellitus.

The common Risk Factors in a person which make him prone for Diabetes are:

1. **Overweight and obesity**. People who are overweight tend to develop diabetes. People who are obese in the middle - around the abdomen (truncal or central obesity) are more prone to develop diabetes in later stages.
2. **Family history**. A family history of diabetes often is an important factor. If both the parents are diabetic, then the chance of developing diabetes is much higher in the children.
3. **Sedentary lifestyle**. Decrease in physical activity with lack of exercise and a sedentary lifestyle are contributors to developing diabetes in later life.
4. **Age**. As age advances, the chance of developing diabetes increases.
5. **Race and Ethnicity**. This contributes to the propensity to develop diabetes. In the US diabetes prevalence is lowest in the

Alaskan natives the prevalence being only 5.5% where in non-Hispanic whites it is 7.1% , non-Hispanic blacks it is 13% and in Native Americans it is the highest at 33%.

6. **Pre-Diabetes**. This is a condition where the blood sugar is higher than normal but not high enough to be diagnosed diabetic. These persons are much more prone to become diabetic in later life .

7. **Diabetes in Pregnancy**. Also called *'Gestational Diabetes'*, females with diabetes which develops during pregnancy, are more prone to diabetes in later life. Women who give birth to overweight babies like e.g., 9 lbs, are prone for diabetes.

8. **Polycystic Ovary Syndrome**. It is a hormonal disorder of the ovaries seen in women of reproductive age. These women tend to become diabetic at a later age in life.

9. **Damage to pancreas**. Certain viruses, toxins, dietary constituents, or chemicals may damage the insulin producing cells of the pancreas leading to diabetes.

How does the physician diagnose Diabetes mellitus.

The diagnosis of diabetes is mainly by checking the levels of sugar (glucose) in blood. The following are the criteria to say that a person is diabetic.

If the blood sugar after 8 hours of fasting is less than 100 mg/100 ml, it is normal.

If the blood sugar checked at any time (Random) is over 200 mg / 100 ml of blood, the person is diabetic.

If the fasting blood sugar is between 100 – 125 mg/100 ml, the person is said to be Pre-Diabetic.

Diabetes mellitus is confirmed if the fasting blood Sugar is above 126 mg/100 ml.

Result	Blood Sugar (mg/100 ml	Diagnosis
Random Blood Sugar	More than 200	Diabetes mellitus
Fasting blood Sugar	More than 126	Diabetes mellitus
Fasting blood sugar	Between 100 – 125	Pre-Diabetes

Another test for diabetes is testing the amount of glucose attached to the hemoglobin in the red blood cells in blood. Hemoglobin is the protein that transports oxygen in the blood. Hemoglobin which has glucose attached to it is called 'Glycated Hemoglobin' and is designated as 'HbA1c' or 'A1C'. the A1C level in blood gives the average value of blood sugar during the past three months (90 days) and is an important index of high blood sugar that the doctors test. A1C is expressed as a percentage. Based on A1C, the patient can be classified as follows.

Result	A1C (%)
Normal	Less than 5.7
Pre-Diabetes	5.7 – 6.4
Diabetes	More than 6.5

Another test the doctor may perform is called the *Oral Glucose Tolerance Test*. In this test, first the blood is drawn after an 8-hour fasting period for testing the blood sugar level. Then the patient is given a sweet drink containing 75 grams of glucose. Blood is drawn again after 2 hours. If the blood shows a glucose value above 200 mg/100 ml after 2 hours, the patient is diabetic. If the value is between 140-200 mg/100 ml, he is diagnosed to have Pre-Diabetes.

When will you check blood sugar in a normal person

Checking blood sugar routinely in normal individuals is done as part of a medical checkup. This is done to detect diabetes early and is done as follows.

- If a person has a Body Mass Index above 25 (23 for Asians)
- If a person is over 35 years – 3 yearly

- If a woman has had Gestational Diabetes (GDM) – 3 yearly
- If a person has been diagnosed Pre-Diabetic – Every year
- All women planning pregnancy , especially with risk factors.
- First prenatal visit of every pregnant woman
- GDM screening at 24-28 weeks of pregnancy.

Body Mass Index (BMI) is a number that denotes the fatness of an individual. It does not give the amount of fat in the person but is an indicator of overweight or obesity of the individual. It is a weight-to-height ratio. It is calculated by dividing the **Weight (in Kilograms) by the square of the Height (in Meters).** It can also be calculated by dividing the **weight in pounds divided by the square of the height in inches multiplied by a conversion factor of 703.**

BMI = Weight (in Kilograms)

Height^2 (in Meters) or

= Weight (in Pounds) x 703

Height ^{2} (in Inches)

Individuals are classified on the basis of the BMI into the following categories.

Category	BMI-Value
Normal	Less than 18.5
Healthy Weight	18.5 – 24.9
Overweight	25-29.9
Obesity	More than 30

Note: In Asian individuals, a BMI of over **23** is considered as overweight instead of 25.

Pre-diabetic state does not necessarily mean that the person will become diabetic in future. Good lifestyle habits and adequate exercise can prevent diabetes from developing in people with Pre-diabetes.

How is Diabetes mellitus treated

The aims of treatment of diabetes are to improve the symptoms of a high blood levels of sugar and to prevent complications of the disease. The treatment of diabetes can be divided into General Measures and Treatment with medications.

General Measures

A healthy lifestyle is the mainstay in the management of DM. Healthy eating, Weight management, Exercise, are some of the general measures adopted.

1. *Healthy Eating – Diet in diabetes.*

The diet for the elderly patients with diabetes will have to be tailored to their needs. The diet will differ from patient to patient depending on his age, lifestyle, culture, personal circumstances, habits, and taste for certain foods. Hence the help of a dietician is needed for prescribing a diet for the patient. However, the general principles regarding the diet of diabetics are as follows:

- Carbohydrates in food determines a patient's blood sugar after a meal. Not more than 50% of the food intake should be from carbohydrates and 10% or less should be from direct table sugar, honey or jaggery.
- Protein intake should form 10 -15% of the intake which roughly works out to 50 grams or 1 mg/kg body weight of the individual.
- The fat in the diet should not exceed 35% of the total intake and of this only 10% or less should be from saturated fat like butter, *ghee*, cheese, cream, coconut, and palm oils.
- The intake of salt should also be restricted to 6 grams per day (1 teaspoonful).
- The food should contain adequate nutrients and vitamins.
- The person should consume at least 5 portions of fruits and vegetables daily.
- It is preferable for the elderly diabetic to take food 5 times a day instead of thrice daily. Breakfast, a mid-morning snack with

coffee or tea, lunch, afternoon snack with tea or coffee and dinner should be served to the patient. The snacks can be one or two non-sweetened biscuits (cookies), or a portion of fruit or nuts.

- The American Diabetic Association recommends that half the plate should be filled with non-starchy vegetables like spinach, carrots, or tomatoes, one fourth with protein foods like tuna, lean meat, chicken, or tofu and one fourth plate with brown rice or starchy vegetables. Appropriate changes should be made for vegetarians and vegans.
- The patient should eat the right amount of food daily and similar portions of food should be taken. The meals should be consumed at almost the same time every day especially when the patient is on medications like insulin.
- It is unsafe for a patient with diabetes to skip a meal as this may lead to low blood sugars and its complications.

What type of foods are ideal for a diabetic

Given below are some of the items of food that are ideal for diabetics. It has to be remembered that some patients prefer to be *vegetarians* and others *vegans* (do not eat animal products or dairy) and hence their diet should be modified accordingly.

- Fruits – Apples, Oranges, Berries, Melon, Pears, Peaches.
- Vegetables – Broccoli, Carrots, Spinach, Zucchini, Cucumber. Starchy vegetables like Potato, Squash, Root vegetables and Corn are lower in carbohydrates than refined grains like rice and wheat. They are, however, a good source of nutrients and may be used in moderation.
- Whole grains – Quinoa, Oats, Brown rice
- Legumes – Beans, Lentils, Chickpeas, Edamame, Soya
- Nuts – Almonds, Walnuts, Pistachios, Cashew, Peanuts.
- Protein rich foods – Skinless poultry, Sea food, Lean cuts of red meat, Tofu, Paneer, Egg white.
- Beverages – Black coffee, Vegetable juice, Unsweetened tea.

Foods which are better avoided or taken sparingly are as follows:

- High fat meat, Fatty cuts of pork, beef and lamb, Dark meat,
- Full fat dairy like whole milk, butter, cheese, and curds.
- Sweets like candies, desserts, cake, ice cream, cookies, baked goods
- Sweeteners like table sugar, honey, jaggery, maple syrup.

- Processed foods like chips, processed meat, packaged food.
- Trans fat containing foods like fried foods, vegetable shortening, margarine, hydrogenated fats and oils, coffee creamers.
- Refined grain products like White rice, *Maida*, White bread, White pasta, breakfast cereals.

Heart healthy foods that a diabetic can take. What to avoid.

- Foods that contain Mono- and Poly-unsaturated fats are ideal for heart health. They are available in Avocado, Nuts, Seeds, Fatty fish like Tuna, Salmon, Sardines and Mackerel. They are named Omega-3-fatty acids. They are also available from soyabean products and tofu. Oils like Olive oil, Canola oil, Corn oil, Peanut oil, Sunflower oil, and Saffola oil contain these fatty acids.
- Saturated fats as are available in Lard, High fat meat, Sausage, Bacon, Hotdogs, Cream, Whole milk, Full fat cheese, Butter, Coconut and Palm oils, Margarine and Hydrogenated fats are better avoided.

- Snacks containing Trans Fats are also to be avoided for a heart healthy diet.- Processed Snacks, Stick margarines, Shortening. Fries

2. *Weight Management*

A higher percentage of elderly patients with diabetes tend to be overweight or obese. In addition, insulin tends to increase the individual's weight. Central obesity with increase in the waist circumference is seen in these individuals.

Managing overweight is important in the general management of diabetes. The patient's BMI has to be checked and a proper diet prescribed to reduce his weight gradually over a period of time.

It is important to reduce the weight of the patient without compromising the nutrient value of the food. A gradual reduction of weight should be aimed for and not crash dieting. A daily reduction of about 600 – 700 Calories from his normal intake achieves this over a period of months. Further, exercise along with this augments the weight loss. The advice of a dietician will be needed in many patients. Adequate vitamin and mineral supplementation will be required. It has to be emphasized here that there is no role for 'starvation diets' in diabetes, especially in the elderly individuals as this can lead to problems like disturbances of sodium and other electrolytes, loss of muscle mass, irregular heartbeat and rarely death.

In rare instances, medications to reduce weight or surgical measures to reduce weight (*Bariatric Surgery*) may be needed to manage obesity.

3. *Exercise in Diabetes*

Diabetics should undertake regular exercise. A structured exercise program may be prescribed for them. The exercise should be regular and sustained. The participation in regular physical activity improves the blood sugar levels, prevents, or delays the onset of diabetes in adults and those in the Pre-diabetic range, positively affects the fats in blood, blood pressure, cardiac events, quality of life and mortality. All diabetics should be encouraged to avoid a sedentary life style and engage in physical activity.

What are the immediate effects of exercise.

- During exercise, the muscles, especially the large muscles of the body take up glucose for energy generation. The intensity and duration of exercise directly increases the amount of glucose burnt. This tends to reduce the blood glucose levels. This reduction remains so for hours even after the person has stopped exercising. Insulin in the body helps the muscles to take up glucose and convert it to energy.

- During exercise, the liver increases the production of glucose and this reduces the glucose stores in the liver also.
- The blood levels remain lower in persons even 24 hours after exercise.
- A combination of Aerobic and Resistance exercises is more effective than either alone.
- Exercises like Yoga and Tai-chi also give similar results to other aerobic exercises.

What are the long-term effects of exercising

- A chronic exercise regimen increases the effectiveness of insulin (*Insulin Sensitivity*) and reduces *insulin resistance*.
- Regular exercise tends to increase the muscle mass of the individual and more muscle in turn can increase the glucose taken up by the muscles.
- The muscles also start to use fat for energy generation leading to reduction of fat in the body.
- Regular exercise tends to reduce the level of 'Bad Cholesterol' (*LDL*) in blood and increase the levels of 'Good Cholesterol' (*HDL*) in blood.

- A slight reduction in blood pressure has been noticed in regular exercisers.
- Death due to diseases of the heart and blood vessels is noted to be less in those who exercise regularly.
- Regular exercise helps in reducing and maintaining the weight of the individual.
- In normal adults with risk factors for diabetes like a strong family history and in Pre-diabetic individuals, exercise prevents or delays the onset of diabetes.
- Regular exercise has its psychological benefits too. The quality of life of the individual improves, depressive symptoms are reduced, and there is a psychological well-being. It improves memory, improves the sleep pattern of the patient, and is said to make the patient feel happier.

Caution. However, if the patient is beginning to exercise for the first time, the elderly person should have a pre-exercise medical evaluation done by a physician to rule out any adverse effects which may occur by undertaking the exercise regimen. The evaluation considers the age of the patient, the duration of diabetes, presence of joint or muscle problems, additional risk factors if any etc. The physician may ask for a full evaluation of the heart with an ECG and Echocardiography if he feels so.

What exercises should a diabetic do

The types of exercises recommended for a diabetic are given below. According to the age and convenience, the patient may undertake whichever exercise regimen that suits him. However, a combination of these exercises is recommended for optimum benefit.

Aerobic Exercise. "Aerobic" means, 'with oxygen'. It means that breathing controls the amount of oxygen that reaches the muscles. This type of exercise mainly improves cardiovascular conditioning. Examples of aerobic exercise include brisk walking, swimming, cycling, rowing, dancing etc.

The recommendation is that at least 150 minutes of aerobic exercise per week should be done. This can be 30 minutes daily for at least 5 days a week. Alternatively short periods of aerobic exercise of 10 minutes each for 3 to 4 times a day can be done.

The exercises should be of moderate intensity. Always start slow and increase the speed of the exercise as days go by. One should always warm up for five minutes before the exercise and cool down at the end.

Resistance Exercise. In this, the muscles are made to contract against an external resistance leading to increase in strength, size, and power of the muscles. The muscles are made to work against a force or weight. Gym based exercises and home-based resistance exercises may be done. Ideally, they should be supervised initially by a competent person or trainer. Free weights like dumbbells, barbells or kettlebells can be used. Resistance bands ('Theraband') which provide resistance during stretch may be used. They are simple, need no complicated equipment and can be carried anywhere by the patient during travel. They are available in various colors according to the resistance offered. One's own weight can also be used for resistance as in pushups or squats.

It is recommended that Resistance training be done at least twice a week on non-consecutive days. The exercises should involve major groups of muscles of the upper and lower body and the core muscles of the body. Usually, 10-15 repetitions are enough to improve muscle power, tone, and strength.

Balance Exercises. Balance control is needed for a person to move independently without fear of falling. This ability decreases with aging and in diabetics due to involvement of the nervous system, this may be impaired further. Hence exercises to improve balance become important especially to prevent falls.

These are simple exercises. Standing on one leg, tandem walking, rising from a chair without holding to the armrest, and squats are some of the balance exercises. Some patients may need to hold on to a chair or the wall initially while training. Yoga exercises also incorporate balance training in them. These are simple exercises and can be done at home. They are useful in diabetics with involvement of the nerves (*polyneuropathy*).

Flexibility Training. Improving the flexibility of joints is also an important part of exercising. This prevents injury and falls in the elderly. Stretching of various muscle groups should be performed. It is better to perform these exercises under supervision initially. They can be performed at home. Yoga and Tai-chi offer excellent flexibility exercises.

Daily activities. In addition to the structured exercise regimens, the person should be encouraged to be as active as possible during the day. Using the stairs instead of the elevator, walking to the nearby store, walking the dog, gardening, standing up and switching on the TV or fan are simple chores where the person is encouraged to be active throughout the day. The sedentary time should be reduced. The person should be encouraged to get up and walk if he is sitting for long. A 15-minute walk after meals is beneficial.

To motivate the individual to move and exercise, there are apps available which can be downloaded into their mobile phones. These apps measure the number of steps taken per day. Smart watches are also available which can keep record of the daily step count.

Some Practical Tips on Exercising.

- Choose some exercise which you enjoy and like. A friend or a partner helps to keep company and provide motivation during the exercise.
- Have a smart goal when you exercise – time the duration or fix the number of steps you will take each day.
- Have a regular schedule for your exercise. Some persons find it easier to exercise in the morning hours whereas others may prefer the evening.
- Do not exercise in the hot sun.
- Drink plenty of liquids while exercising.
- Wear shoes that are properly fitting and comfortable. Use cotton dress and socks. Avoid tight fitting clothes while exercising.
- Wash your feet after exercising and check your feet for any sores or injuries frequently.

4. Other Measures

Alcohol, in excess can make diabetes haywire and hence should be avoided or taken only in moderation. People who drink may not take adequate food and are prone to develop low blood sugar (*Hypoglycemia*) which can be dangerous. Alcohol also has a high calorie content and can lead to overweight or obesity.

Ramadan fasting is a requirement for Muslims. The person has to take special precautions to prevent low blood sugar values during fasting. The patient's physician should be consulted prior to the Ramadan month and adequate changes in the dose and timing of the medications should be made. Often the doctor would prefer to add medications which are less prone to cause low blood sugar or hypoglycemia.

The diabetic patients who are on Insulin for controlling blood sugar should be careful while driving as sudden low blood sugars can lead to confusion and even loss of consciousness

Medications to treat Diabetes

Oral medications and Insulin are the mainstay in the treatment of diabetes. The dose of the medication is individualized. *'One size does not fit all'* is the dictum in prescribing medications for diabetes. The physician managing the person will decide on the appropriate medications depending on the lifestyle of the patient, his educational status, his employment, body weight etc.

Oral medications of various types are available and should be taken strictly as per the advice of the physician. Similarly, Insulin has to be taken by injection and the patient must be trained to administer the injection by himself. In circumstances where the patient cannot inject himself as in dementia, poor eyesight, confusion or paralysis, the patient's caregiver should administer the insulin injection daily at the appropriate time of the day. Timing of food intake is also important when administering the Insulin injection. Insulin shots are ideally taken 20 – 30 minutes before a meal.

Special Considerations in Elderly Individuals with Diabetes

The complications occurring in diabetes are the same for elderly individuals as compared to the younger patients. However, in patients in whom diabetes begins later in life, the complications may take longer to develop and hence may be lower in incidence. But due to the advanced age, other co-existing illnesses in the elderly may increase complications like heart disease, eye complications etc.

The main problems specifically encountered in old age are as follows:

- Elderly individuals are more prone to acute decrease in blood sugar (*Hypoglycemia*). This may lead to giddiness and falls, confusion and even loss of consciousness. Other symptoms of hypoglycemia are weakness, severe sweating, palpitations, delirium, confusion, and bizarre behaviour.

- An acute increase in blood sugar (*Hyperglycemia*) can also occur in the elderly diabetic. This can lead to increase in urination resulting in dehydration and subsequent decrease in blood pressure. This may also lead to giddiness and make the patient prone to falls. The symptoms are atypical compared to that in younger adults and may be mistaken for a neurological disease. Hence the recognition of hyperglycemia in the elderly may be delayed and treatment not given in time. Any change in the behaviour or mental status of a diabetic elderly patient should necessitate immediate checking of the blood sugar.

- The management of co-existing conditions like high blood pressure, heart disease, high blood cholesterol or kidney disease is very important in the elderly and the medications should be regularly taken.

- The A1C goal is set a bit higher in elderly individuals as a strict control of blood sugar is not needed as this can lead to sudden hypoglycemia. Hence in elderly diabetics the A1C is generally kept between 7 - 7.5%.

- In the elderly it should be remembered that the A1C levels may not accurately reflect the 3-monthly blood sugar values as the presence of co-existing diseases like kidney disease, heart disease and high blood pressure can give falsely high or low A1C values.

- The presence of cognitive decline and neurological abnormalities in the elderly may pose problems in managing diabetes in them.
- It is to be remembered that elderly patients with diabetes are more prone to heart attacks and any symptoms out of the ordinary should be taken seriously. (See section on *Heart Attack*).
- The elderly should be encouraged to undertake physical activity frequently instead of prolonged periods of exercise.
- The nutritional status of the diabetic elderly patient should be given adequate consideration as their food intake may be restricted or impaired due to various problems like poor dental hygiene, poor dentition, swallowing difficulties, alteration in functions of the intestines, changes in taste perception, co-existing illnesses, and consequent diet restrictions. The diet for the elderly diabetic should be tailored to their individual needs.
- Elderly diabetics may find it difficult to take injections of Insulin by themselves due to various causes like poor eyesight, memory impairment, arthritis of the fingers leading to difficulty in loading the syringe and injecting themselves. They should be helped by the caregiver or relative.

Complications of Diabetes

Diabetes is a disease with many varied facets of presentations and its complications are highly damaging to various organs of the body. The elderly diabetics are more prone for complications as age is a risk factor in many of the complications that occur. There are some complications of diabetes which produce abrupt changes. These are called the Acute Complications and those that produce changes gradually over a period of time, are called the Chronic Complications.

Let us discuss some of the Acute complications of diabetes.

Acute complications of Diabetes.

There are three main acute complications of diabetes which can be dangerous. They are Diabetic ketoacidosis, Very high blood glucose and Very low blood glucose. They are discussed below:

Diabetic Ketoacidosis. (DK)

This is an acute complication of diabetes which is dangerous and can be fatal if not treated in time. When the person's blood sugar is very high, acidic substances and ketones increase in the blood. This occurs when enough insulin is not available in the body either from the patient's pancreas or administered by injection. As insulin is needed for converting glucose into energy, its scarcity leads to breaking down of fat in the body to release energy. This releases the dangerous chemicals, ketones into blood which increase the acid content of blood leading to the complication.

DK can be caused when the patient misses his insulin dose or takes inadequate doses of insulin. Infections or other illnesses in the body may increase the chances of this complication.

The symptoms are usually increase in the frequency of urination, dry mouth, extreme thirst, dehydration, a very high blood glucose and high levels of ketones detected in urine. Nausea, vomiting and pain in the abdomen are often present. The patient has a dry skin, breathes rapidly, and is often confused. If left untreated it leads to loss of consciousness and coma. Death may occur. The breath of the patient has a fruity smell to it.

DK is a medical emergency and immediate hospitalization with administration of fluids through the veins and injections of insulin are needed for its control.

Prevention of DK is by adequate control of blood glucose levels, adjusting the dose of insulin needed for the patient, eating meals at the proper times, prompt treatment of all infections and fevers, and consulting the doctor if any of the symptoms are suspected.

Hyperglycemia. Very high blood glucose is called '*Hyperglycemia*'. It can occur in the following situations.

- An acute increase in blood sugar can occur if the patient skips his dose of medications or insulin.
- Indulgence in food without control e.g., if the patient takes plenty of sweet snacks or carbohydrates.
- The presence of any infection can lead to hyperglycemia.
- Not taking the injection of insulin correctly as per the doctor's advice or using expired insulin medication may also cause hyperglycemia.
- A sedentary lifestyle increases the chances of hyperglycemia.
- If steroids are given to the patient for any disease like asthma, it can cause hyperglycemia.
- Hyperglycemia can also occur during stress, surgery, or emotional trauma.

The patient feels intensely thirsty, passes urine frequently, has dry mouth and skin, feels excessively tired, is confused or delirious and rarely may go into a coma. This condition is called '*Hyperosmolar Hyperglycemic Syndrome*. This occurs usually when the level of blood glucose is over **600 mg/ 100 ml**. If left uncorrected, it may lead to diabetic ketoacidosis. Prompt insulin injection to bring down the blood sugar is the treatment given. **Hypoglycemia.** Contrary to high blood glucose, very low blood glucose is called '*Hypoglycemia*' and is often due to blood glucose levels below **70 mg/100 ml.** Hypoglycemia can occur under the following

- Low blood glucose can be due to skipping of meals while taking the medications or insulin.
- Inadvertently taking a higher dose of insulin or oral medication for diabetes. Patients with cognitive disorders may forget to have taken the medication already and take a repeat dose unknowingly leading to hypoglycemia.
- Alcohol intake without eating any food along with it.
- Exercising on an empty stomach.

Elderly diabetics are prone for hypoglycemia and this may be very serious in them as their symptoms may be masked and the diagnosis missed. The relatives or caregivers of the elderly patient should be familiar with the symptoms of hypoglycemia so that prompt recognition is possible.

The symptoms the patient presents with are often trembling, sweating, pale face, irresistible hunger, irritability, confusion, dizziness, difficulty to concentrate, and occasionally slurring of speech. It has to be specifically noted that alcohol can precipitate hypoglycemia in diabetics if they do not eat food along with alcohol. *The symptoms of hypoglycemia might, hence, be mistaken for alcoholic drunkenness. The patient may be diagnosed as drunk and the hypoglycemia missed.* Hence, in any diabetic patient who presents with such symptoms but with the smell of alcohol in his breath, the blood sugar should be immediately checked. In severe cases the patient may have fits resembling epilepsy. The severity of sweating may give the impression that the patient is having a heart attack. This is also often accompanied by palpitations of the heart.

Once the symptoms are detected early, the patient should be given some glucose containing item like candy, fruit juice or anything sweet. This can relieve the symptoms immediately. This should be followed up with a carbohydrate meal.

Severe cases call for immediate medical attention. Glucose has to be injected through the vein and other medications to increase the blood glucose levels would have to be given. This medication is called *Glucagon* and acts to increase the blood sugar by releasing glucose from the liver. The patient should also be evaluated as to the cause of hypoglycemia and this should be corrected.

Chronic Complications of Diabetes.

In addition to the acute complications, diabetes can affect almost every organ and system in the body and cause long term complications which occur gradually over a period of time and if not treated promptly or prevented, can lead to serious trouble for the patient.

The long term or chronic complications are discussed below.

Heart Disease . There are many risk factors for the causation of heart disease, and diabetes is one of them. In fact, diabetes increases the risk due to all the other risk factors in causing heart disease. The large blood vessels in the body are also affected by diabetes. Coronary artery disease is the most dreaded complication of diabetes leading to heart attacks and chest pain on effort, named *Angina Pectoris*. Heart attacks are twice higher in diabetics compared to non-diabetics. All the conventional risk factors like high blood pressure, smoking, sedentary habits, obesity, and high blood cholesterol can additionally increase the risk of heart disease in the diabetic. (See section on *Heart Attack*)

Stroke. Stroke is due to the disease affecting the blood vessels supplying the brain.

(See section on *Stroke*). Stroke was noted to be 1.5 times higher in diabetics compared to non-diabetics.

Kidney disease. Chronic kidney disease occurs in long standing diabetes. in the US 1 in 3 patients with diabetes have kidney disease. Chronic kidney disease leading to need for dialysis occurs later in the disease. The elderly patients are more prone to develop kidney disease. Diabetes damages the nephrons which are the filtering units of the kidney and also the blood vessels which supply blood to the kidneys. Increase in blood pressure also damages the kidney over time. In addition, recurrent urinary tract infections are also a frequent complication of diabetes. (See section on *Chronic Kidney Disease*)

High Blood Pressure. Two out of three patients with diabetes have high blood pressure. High BP is in turn a risk factor in causing heart disease.

Eye Damage. The eye complications of diabetes are Diabetic retinopathy, glaucoma, and cataract. Unchecked, this can lead to serious visual impairment or even blindness.

Retinal Damage. The retina is the layer of light sensitive cells at the back inside the eye. It acts as a screen on which the images which we see fall. The retina is supplied by thin delicate hair-like blood vessels (capillaries) which can be damaged in diabetes. this is called '*Diabetic Retinopathy*'. The symptoms are blurring of vision, difficulty in identifying colors, occasional flashes of light, distortion of images or dark areas in the visual field. Total loss of vision may occur in the late stages of the disease.

Glaucoma. Glaucoma is an increase in pressure inside the eyeball and is a complication of diabetes. It affects vision, causing severe headache, seeing halos around the lights, redness of eyes and later can damage the nerve to the eyeball (*Optic Nerve*) thus compromising vision.

Cataracts. Cataract is a condition where the transparent lens in the eye gradually becomes opaque thus impairing vision. Cataracts develop in diabetics at an earlier age than in non-diabetic populations. Symptoms of cataract are gradual impairment of vision.

Prevention of eye complications are by avoiding smoking, controlling blood sugar, controlling high BP, regular exercise, keeping blood cholesterol under control, and avoiding other risk factors. Once a year a checkup with the eye doctor (*Ophthalmologist*) is necessary.

Nerve Complications. Long standing diabetes damages the nerves in various parts of the body. This is called *'Diabetic Neuropathy'*.

- When the nerves in the upper and lower limbs are affected the patient feels a tingling sensation in the feet and legs and occasionally the hands and forearms. They feel 'pins and needles' in the feet and legs. Occasionally they feel pain or numbness in the limbs. When the nerve damage is severe, the patient may not feel pain in the feet and this can be dangerous as pain is a protective sensation and lack of pain can make a person unaware of any damage or injury to the feet. Painless ulcers and blisters may develop in the feet which can lead to complications like diabetic foot.
- When the nerves to the bowels and bladder are involved, the patient may have constipation, diarrhea, or vomiting.
- Involvement of the nerves to the sex organs, causes difficulty in erection and ejaculation in males, and dryness of vagina, pain during sexual intercourse or inability to feel orgasm in females.
- When the nerves to the muscles of the thigh, buttocks or arms are involved, there may be weakness of these muscles causing difficulty in getting up from sitting posture, raising one's arms, or pain in these muscles on walking or during exercise.

- Involvement of the muscles moving the eye weakens them, causing double vision and inability to move the eyeball.
- When muscles of the face are involved, the patient may have paralysis of one half of the face with inability to close the eyelids or have drooping of the angle of the mouth. This condition is called *Bell's Palsy*.

Oral health. Lack of good oral hygiene and care of gums and teeth can lead to poor oral health in diabetics. Increase in sugar levels in blood also increases the sugar in saliva. This leads to harmful bacteria multiplying in the mouth leading to cavities, tooth decay and gum disease. Loss of teeth may occur. The gums may be swollen, infected and may bleed occasionally.

Brushing one's teeth twice daily with a fluoride containing toothpaste using a soft brush, flossing once or twice a day, quitting smoking, rinsing one's mouth after or taking food or drinking any liquid except water are some of the preventive measures to maintain good oral health. In the elderly, loss of teeth and gum disease occurring in diabetes can lead to poor feeding and poor nutrition. Regular visits to the dentist once or twice a year is necessary. Whenever needed, properly fitting dentures should be provided to the patient.

Hearing Loss. Age itself leads to hearing loss. Diabetes can damage the nerves in the inner ear and cause loss of hearing. Strict control of blood sugar, yearly checkup with an ENT specialist, avoiding loud noises especially when using the earphones are some methods of preventing hearing loss. There are some medications like certain antibiotics, medicines given for heart diseases, aspirin in high doses and some pain killers which can impair hearing. One should discuss with one's physician regarding the use of these medications.

Mental Health.   Mental health is as important as physical health for the elderly diabetic. Our feelings and thoughts can affect our body's health too. The body and the mind are closely connected. Diabetics are prone to certain problems of mental health more commonly than non-diabetics.

Depression. Diabetic patients are 2 – 3 times more likely to be depressed than normal people. The elderly diabetics are especially more prone to this complication as they may be lonely and living independently away from their near and dear ones. The symptoms which point to depression are, a feeling of sadness, loss of interest in surroundings or avoiding even their normal routine activities, increased sleep, or lack of sleep, overeating or starving, not able to concentrate and not able to take decisions on even simple matters. Occasionally the patient may have thoughts of death or suicide. Many elders with depression go undiagnosed and unrecognized and live miserably with this problem.

Anxiety and Stress. Even though stress is part of normal life, the diabetic elderly individual may feel extremely stressed at times and unable to tackle even the normal day to day problems. An empathetic approach on the part of the close relatives and the caregiver are needed to manage this.

To keep normal mental health and prevent illness, the elderly diabetic should be encouraged to exercise, move with friends or in groups, get enough sleep, avoid alcohol and caffeine in excess and keep oneself engaged in some activity or hobby which they find enjoyable. When living with close kith and kin, the diabetic elders should be included in the conversations and decision making, so that they feel and integral part of the family and do not feel 'left out'.

Skin complications. Various skin complications are noted in long standing diabetes. Often they are ignored by the elderly diabetic and detected accidentally by the relatives or the caregiver. Some of these problems are as follows:

- Black, velvety patches may be noticed in the armpits, groin and around the neck. They are called *'Acanthosis nigricans'*.
- The skin in the back of the hand may look shiny, tight, and thick.
- Skin infections especially with fungus may occur in the armpits or groins. Good hygiene is needed to prevent this. There may be infection around the nail of the finger or toe with pus formation in some. This is called *Paronychia* and is common.
- Diabetic ulcers may occur in the legs and they do not heal quickly. They may become chronic leading to *gangrene* and may eventually need amputation of the foot or leg if severe.
- The patient may have dry itchy skin lesions especially in the legs. This is due to the lack of moisture in the skin and also to poor blood circulation in the legs due to disease of the blood vessels.
- Blisters and cracks may occur in the feet and legs which may ultimately lead to ulcers.
- Flat yellowish patches may occur around the eyes in some. They are called *'Xanthelasma'*. They are due to cholesterol deposits under the skin and are harmless more of a cosmetic concern.

Prevention of Skin complications

Good hygiene especially of the creases of the body, keeping the skin moist, bathing regularly, avoiding excess use of soap and application of oil or a moisturizing cream to the skin especially of the legs after bath are effective strategies in preventing skin problems. The skin around the genitals should be kept clean and dry. Blood sugar should be well controlled and regular exercises improve the blood flow to the skin. In winter, one should avoid sitting close to the room heater to prevent overheating and dryness of the skin of the legs and feet. Consultation with a skin specialist is needed when any changes are noticed in the skin.

Diabetic Foot. The feet are a common site where problems occur in the diabetic. Foot care hence is of paramount importance. The elderly especially may find it difficult to care for their feet as they may not be able to bend forward to inspect their feet or may be hampered by poor vision.

Two main complications of diabetes cause foot problems. These are complications affecting the nerves and those affecting the blood vessels thereby reducing the blood supply to the feet. These cause the 'diabetic foot'. The patient may not feel sensation in the feet and hence small injuries may go unnoticed and lead to more severe complications like blisters and ulcers. As the patient does not feel pain sensation in the joints, the joints may deform leading to crippling disabilities.

The poor blood flow can ultimately lead to **Gangrene**. This indicates death of skin, muscle, and tissues in the feet. The skin becomes blue or black in color and is swollen. The gangrene may get infected leading to a foul-smelling discharge from the site of infection. This may ultimately cause that part of the foot to be removed by surgery – called 'amputation'. Gangrene is a very dangerous condition and if the infection from a gangrene spreads to the blood, it can cause serious infection which may lead to death.

What can be done to prevent 'Diabetic Foot'

Foot hygiene is a very important aspect of the management of diabetes, especially in the elderly population which may be affected with arthritis, muscle weakness, poor vision, and inability to take care of oneself. Often they may require the help of a caregiver or relative to care for their feet. The following preventive measures are advocated.

- The patient's feet and soles should be inspected daily by himself or by a caregiver for cuts, bruises, injuries, blisters etc. Any cuts should be covered with a band-aid.
- The feet should be washed with soap and warm water and dried daily. Following this,

moisturizing lotion must be applied to the feet. The lotion should not be applied between the toes as this area should be kept dry.

- Toe nails should be cut or filed straight across.
- Corns and calluses should be removed by a doctor or a podiatrist. The patient should not be allowed to do it himself. Over the counter remedies to remove them should not be used.
- The patient should wear suitable well-fitting shoes.. Cotton socks should be worn with shoes.
- The patient should never go barefoot even indoors. Socks should be changed daily. The inside of shoes should be inspected before wearing them for any loose pebbles or other material which can injure the feet.
- Special footwear is available for diabetics and this may be chosen depending on the advice of the doctor or podiatrist.
- Woolen socks should be worn to warm the feet in winter.
- Bare feet should not be placed near the heater or fire to warm them.
- The feet should be put up on a footstool or ottoman while sitting. Toes should be wiggled often. The patient should be encouraged to walk around frequently to increase the blood flow to the feet and legs.

- The doctor should be requested to inspect the feet at every visit.

HYPOTHYROIDISM

In the elderly, decrease in thyroid function named *'Hypothyroidism'* is common as age produces immune changes which affect thyroid function. It is more common in women. Often the symptoms may be missed as they may be nonspecific and masked by the presence of other co-existing illnesses in the elderly individual.

In the United States, the prevalence of Hypothyroidism in adults has been found to vary from 0.2-3.7% of the population. Subclinical Hypothyroidism, where the symptoms are minimal and only the blood shows mildly positive tests for the disease is seen in a higher percentage of population 1.5-12.5%. In India hypothyroidism is reported approximately in 1 out of 10 adults. In Europe the prevalence is reported to be 0.2 – 5.3% of the adult population. A study from Colorado in the US among 25000 adults revealed that 10% of men and 16% of women between the ages of 65 and 74 had increase in Thyroid Stimulating Hormone (TSH) which is an indicator of hypothyroidism. Over the age of 75 it was present in 16% of men and 21% of women. This only goes to show that hypothyroidism is not a rare disorder.

Causes of Hypothyroidism

The disease is due to the decrease in the hormone named *Thyroxine* produced by the thyroid gland. This decrease occurs as the patient ages. There are many causes of hypothyroidism. Some of the causes are given below.

- Iodine deficiency can lead to hypothyroidism and is seen to be prevalent in hilly areas of the countries where the salt (unlike sea salt) is deficient in iodine. The patients may have swelling of the thyroid gland, a condition called '**Goiter**'.
- Autoimmune diseases, where the body attacks its own cells, can cause the body to attack the thyroid gland and lead to hypothyroidism. The body manufactures antibodies against the thyroid gland causing it to get damaged.
- Surgery on the thyroid where the gland is removed when there is a tumor.
- Certain medications given for some diseases may produce hypothyroidism.
- Radiation given to the neck for some diseases can lead to hypothyroidism.
- Occasionally hypothyroidism may follow certain acute viral illnesses.

- Hypothyroidism can also occur when there is a decrease in function of the Pituitary Gland (an endocrine gland situated in the brain).

What are the symptoms of Hypothyroidism

There are various symptoms which are subtle and may be nonspecific and hence the diagnosis of the disease may be missed in early stages. The main symptoms which the patients complains of are as follows.

- Tiredness, weight gain, constipation, lack of energy and inability to concentrate are the usual symptoms. The patient may feel depressed and irritable. Muscle weakness occurs in some. Others may have muscle cramps.
- The skin may become dry and itchy. The skin may become thick in late stages, a condition called *'Myxedema'* where the patient's face looks puffy especially around the eyes. The skin may assume a yellow tint.
- The hair is thinned out, coarse and the patient tends to lose hair.
- The patient may feel intolerant to cold. Vague aches and pains are felt in the joints.

- There is a generalized slowness of movement, a sort of sluggishness that the person feels.
- The voice of the patient may change and become hoarse.
- Decrease in taste sensation, hearing loss and impairment of memory may occur in some patients.
- The doctor may find that the blood pressure of the patient may be elevated, his blood levels of cholesterol are often high, and the heart rate may be slow.
- In rare cases of extreme hypothyroidism, the patient may go into coma. This is a medical emergency and is called '**Myxedema Coma**' needing urgent hospitalization and treatment.

The doctor diagnoses hypothyroidism by checking the level of blood hormones. The level of Thyroxine, which is the hormone produced by the thyroid gland is reduced in blood. However, another hormone called the Thyroid Stimulating Hormone (TSH) which is produced by the Pituitary gland in the brain is increased in Hypothyroidism. Detection of an increase in TSH in blood is an important test to diagnose hypothyroidism.

The symptoms of hypothyroidism are often mistaken for the normal changes of old age. Symptoms like hearing impairment, weight gain, depression, sluggishness, tiredness, muscle, and joint pains all may be passed off as normal age-related changes in the patient and hence the diagnosis of hypothyroidism may be missed in the early stages. It is important to have a high degree of suspicion in diagnosing this condition in the elderly. Any change in any of the behaviour or attitude of the elderly patient should be given due consideration and investigated.

Treatment consists of replacing the deficient thyroid hormone – Thyroxine- orally with tablets. In the elderly, the medication has to be started in small doses and gradually increased as per the physician's advice. Other general measures will be needed to control the other associated symptoms in the patient.

HYPERTHYROIDISM

Just like hypothyroidism, overactivity of the thyroid gland with increased secretion of thyroid hormones is called **Hyperthyroidism**. This can cause significant challenges in diagnosis as the symptoms in the elderly individuals may be atypical and less than in the young. The chances of adverse events are also high. The prevalence of hyperthyroidism is quoted to be 0.5 to 4% in various studies.

What are the causes of Hyperthyroidism

The causes of hyperthyroidism are listed below.

- Excess of iodine ingestion can lead to hyperthyroidism. Iodine is present in some cough syrups, certain medications, or used in contrast medium used in radiography. Kelp, dulse, and some seaweeds have high iodine content and may lead to hyperthyroidism.
- Grave's disease is a disease of thyroid where the immune system of the body attacks the thyroid (*autoimmune disease*) and causes it to secrete excess amounts of thyroid hormone.
- An excess of thyroid hormone used in the treatment of hypothyroidism can lead to hyperthyroidism. Hence, the dose of thyroid hormone in treating hypothyroidism should be carefully monitored.
- Inflammation of the thyroid gland, called Thyroiditis can lead to hyperthyroidism.
- Some tumors (lumps) of the thyroid gland can secrete excess amounts of thyroid hormones. These are called Thyroid Nodules.
- Occasionally, thyroid cancer can also cause excess secretion of hormones and hyperthyroidism.

What are the symptoms of Hyperthyroidism

In the elderly, the symptoms of hyperthyroidism may be different from that in the young or only one or two symptoms may be present. The usuals symptoms are as follows:

- Tremors of the hands may be noticed in patients. Their voice also may be tremulous.
- Anxiety may be a symptom in some patients.
- Palpitations may be noticed by patients who have a fast heart rate which is a common occurrence in hyperthyroidism. Their pulse is faster than in normal individuals and may be irregular occasionally if atrial fibrillation is present.
- The patient may not tolerate heat and may feel very uncomfortable in hot surroundings. Excess sweating may occur.
- The patient may lose weight due to hyperthyroidism as the body metabolism in increased.
- In some patients shortness of breath may be noticed as a prominent symptom.
- Some elderly individuals may present with depression and agitation – a condition called *"Apathetic Hyperthyroidism"*. The patient has fatigue, loss of appetite, apathy and occasionally, cognitive decline.

o Weakness of muscles especially of the muscles in the thigh and upper arm are noticed in some patients. This may manifest as difficulty in raising the arms or rising up from the sitting or squatting position.

o Most patients with hyperthyroidism have an increased blood pressure. It is the systolic blood pressure which is raised much more than the diastolic blood pressure (See Section on *High Blood Pressure*).

What complications can occur in Hyperthyroidism

The important complications that occur in hyperthyroidism are as follows:

• Atrial fibrillation is a common in hyperthyroidism. It is an irregular palpitation of the heart. (See section on *Atrial fibrillation*). About 25-30% of individuals with hyperthyroidism develop atrial fibrillation which in turn can lead to stroke. Occasionally, in the elderly, atrial fibrillation may be the only sign of the presence of hyperthyroidism.

• Death due to heart disease is higher in patients with hyperthyroidism.

• Heart failure is another complication of hyperthyroidism.

- Patients with hyperthyroidism are highly prone to develop Osteoporosis which in turn can lead to fractures especially in older women.
- High blood pressure leading to its complications may be seen in many patients.
- Stroke, which is highly disabling may occur as a complication in hyperthyroidism.

How is hyperthyroidism treated.

The excess secretion of the thyroid hormone can be reduced with medications. These are effective in controlling the disease. The dose of the medication should be closely monitored as a high dose may lead to hypothyroidism and its adverse effects.

Other medications like *Beta blockers* are used to control the heart rate in case of fast heart rates caused by the disease, especially in atrial fibrillation. These medications also reduce the tremors, irritability, and anxiety in the patients.

Treating the patient with radioactive iodine compounds is the latest form of therapy. The radioactive iodine causes a controlled destruction of part of the cells in the thyroid gland causing the thyroid to secrete lesser amount of hormone.

When atrial fibrillation is present, it is treated appropriately as described in the section on Atrial Fibrillation. (See the section on *Heart*)

Surgery is another option in the treatment of hyperthyroidism. In the elderly, however, surgery may be contraindicated because of the presence of other co-existing diseases like Diabetes, Heart disease or Stroke. In them it is preferable to use medications to control the disease. During surgery, part or whole of the thyroid gland is removed. The patient is then given small doses of thyroid hormone to keep the blood levels of the hormone normal.

Resources

1. . Davidson's Principles and Practice of Medicine. 23rd. Ed. Elsevier 2018. Chapter 17-Respiratory Medicine, pages 545-628.

2. Diabetes mellitus in the elderly. Chentli.F, AzzougS, Mahgoun.S, Indian J of Endocrinology & Metabolism. 2015, 19: 744-752.

3. CDC 2022 National Diabetes Statistics Report–2022

4. The American Diabetes Association 2022 Standards of Medical Care in Diabetes Update , Feb 23, 2022

5.Exercise & type 2 diabetes. Colberg SR et al. Diabetes Care. 2010. Dec. 33: 147-167

6.Diabetes and Chronic Kidney disease. CDC

7. Approach to and Treatment of Thyroid Disorders in the Elderly. Papaleontiou M and Haymart MR.   Medical Clinics of North America. 2012. Vol. 96: pages 297-310.

8.Hyperthyroidism in Aging. Samuels MH. National Library of Medicine.

9.Hyperthyroidism   (Overactive Thyroid). Mayo Clinic Patient Care and Health Information.

Chapter 6. BONES & JOINTS

Structure & Function. *The skeletal system comprising the bones and the joints along with the muscles attached to them gives shape to the body. It also helps to protect certain organs of the body like the brain (skull), the Lungs and the heart (bones of the chest wall), the liver (ribs) and the spinal cord (Vertebral column). The bones are hollow inside filled with a spongy **marrow** which produces the cells that circulate in blood. The bones are a storehouse of minerals like calcium, phosphorus, Vitamin D and iron.*

*An adult skeleton has 206 bones of various sizes and shapes, each having a function of its own. The bone is covered by a thin tough covering called the **Periosteum**. The bone itself has a compact outer part and a spongy inner part which is filled with marrow.*

*A **Joint** is the junction where two or more bones come together to permit movement. Most of the large joints are movable. Some joints are partly movable, and some joints are immovable. Thick bands of tissue called **Ligaments** hold together the bones that form the joints. **Tendons** are thick bands that firmly anchor the ends of muscles to the bone.* **(See Fig. 8)**

Cartilage is the tissue in the joints between bones that prevents the end of the bones from rubbing together and causing friction. It is a tough rubbery material which acts as a cushion and a shock absorber to prevent damage to the joints. The cartilage protects the ends of the bones and the joints.

The Spine is formed of bones called **Vertebrae**. They are small-sized blocks of bone having a central hole and when they are stacked together, they form a canal in the centre of the vertebral column called the **Spinal canal** which houses the Spinal Cord which is an extension of the brain stem. There are 7 vertebrae which form the neck extending down from the lower surface of the skull. They are called the **Cervical Vertebrae**. There are 12 vertebrae which are seen at the back of the chest. These are the **Thoracic Vertebrae**. The 12 pairs of ribs are attached to them. In the lower back there are 5 vertebrae named the **Lumbar Vertebrae**. They are thicker and bigger than the thoracic vertebrae as they support the lower back.

Below the lumbar vertebrae, there is the **Sacrum** which is a triangular bone formed of 5 fused vertebrae. Below the sacrum is the **Coccyx** or the tiny tailbone, a small vestige of the tail which is absent in humans.

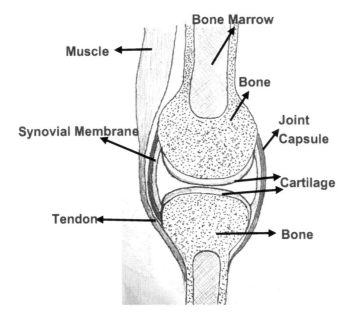

Figure 8. (Joint- Structure)

Diseases and symptoms relating to bones and joints are very important and common as one grows old and this leads to decrease in the quality of life of the person. Osteoarthritis or age-related bone and joint degeneration affects almost 30 million Americans causing variable amounts of disability in them. Falls leading to fractures and dislocations are more important in the elderly. The healing process after a fracture is delayed in the elderly.

What age does to Bones & Joints

The human skeleton has a dual function of giving a structure and form to the human body and also providing support to the attachment of muscles. Normally, joints are cushioned by a padding of cartilage which is like a padding at the end of bones and in joints giving a cushioning effect. It prevents the joints from being damaged by mechanical shocks and acts as a shock absorber. Also, there is an adequate amount of fluid in the joint called the *'synovial fluid'* which acts as a lubricant inside the joints. The muscles of the body are attached to the bones and provide force and strength for the movements of the body. The human posture and locomotion are controlled by the coordinated effort of the bones, muscles and joints controlled overall by the brain and the nervous system.

As age advances changes occur in the bones and joints of the body. The bones lose density as the minerals and calcium in the bone decrease. The spine is a stack of bones called the *'vertebrae'*. These also tend to become less dense and the cartilage between them, called *'Intervertebral discs'* which act as the shock absorbers to the spine, lose their turgid nature and become thinner. The vertebrae also tend to decrease in thickness leading to an overall decrease in height of the individual. It is found that after the age of 30 a person decreases in height by half an inch (1 centimeter) every 10 years. This decreases is faster after the age of 70 and the person may lose as much as one to three inches in height. The long bones of the arms and legs also become thin and brittle but retain their length. The joints also degenerate leading to movement problems in the joints.

The muscles tend to lose the number of cells in them and shrink in size the muscle tissue is replaced by non-elastic tissue. The tone of the muscles also decreases as one ages. The overall muscle mass in the body also decreases.

The individual becomes stooped and his back tends to get bent and shoulders may narrow and droop. The neck may have a forward tilt. Overall, the person's movements are slower and he tends to take shorter steps. The gait also tends to become unsteady. Both the person's endurance and strength are reduced. These changes are unavoidable as the person grows older.

The total quantity of body fat tends to decrease after the age of 30. Men increase their weight till the age of 55. The weight decreases thereafter as the male hormone, testosterone in the body decreases. Women tend to gain weight till the age of 65 and then begin to lose weight. Thus, by the age of 70 to 75, the overall shape of the body changes.

The diseases common in old age are Osteoarthritis, Rheumatoid Arthritis, Osteoporosis.

OSTEOARTHRITIS

Osteoarthritis (OA) is a term used to describe degeneration of the joints of the hands, fingers, ankles, knees, and spine. This tends to occur as the person grows older. OA is said to affect approximately 30 million Americans. The disease creeps on the individual gradually over a period of 10-15 years ultimately disabling many of them. It is the most common disability in old age and affects men and women. Women are four times more prone for OA.

The main change which occurs in the disease is the wear and tear occurring in the cartilages of the joints which act as shock absorbers. The normal amount of lubricant joint fluid present in the joint also decreases so that the bones inside the joints tend to rub against each other and this produces the excruciating pain felt by the individual. The range of movements of the joints also decreases and there may be bony outgrowths known as 'bony spurs' which develop and may be large enough to compress nearby nerves and cause symptoms of nerve pain or muscle weakness.

What are the symptoms of OA

Often the early symptoms are stiffness of the joints which are felt more in the mornings on waking and tend to decrease after some time as the joint movements increase during the day. The pain may vary from mild to severe and excruciating depending on the amount of damage in the joint. A grating feeling is felt when the joints move. Occasionally small bony knobs develop especially on the joints of the fingers. The joints of the hands, wrists, neck, hips, and knees may be affected. The hips, spine and knees being the weight bearing joints are affected much more than those of the upper limbs.

The joints affected may be swollen and warm to touch. Occasionally redness may be seen over the joint. The joints may be painful to touch.

The hands tend to be affected more in the females. The fingers may become gnarled, with enlarged joints and stiffness.

The knees are commonly affected and the person feels stiffness, pain and swelling. Walking becomes difficult. The person finds it very painful and difficult to get up from the sitting posture and needs support to do so. It is often highly disabling.

The hips are affected in some patients causing pain in the inner thighs, and buttocks. Movements like bending forward and putting on shoes become difficult and painful.

OA affecting the spine leads to stiffness and pain in the neck and lower back often. Pressure on nerves which leave through the gaps between the vertebrae, causes nerve pain, numbness, a feeling of pins and needles and at times muscle weakness. When the nerves to the bladder or bowel are affected this may lead to difficulty in passing urine or incontinence of urine and affect bowel function.

What are the causes of OA

The following are some of the causes that lead to OA.

- The <u>stress on joints</u> especially the weight bearing joints leads to OA as the person ages.
- <u>Impaired alignment of the joint</u> as may occur after a fracture heals without proper treatment or in birth defects of the limbs.
- <u>Overweight and obesity</u> are a common cause of OA affecting the weight bearing joints. People carrying heavy loads on their heads tend to develop OA of the vertebrae in the neck in old age. Some women constantly carry heavy hand bags on their shoulders. This can lead to OA of the

shoulders and is called 'Heavy Purse Syndrome".

- Previous injuries to the bone or joint can lead to OA in later age. Sports injuries occurring in early age can cause OA as the person grows old. Stress on joints due to competitive sports, cartilage damage occurring during sports, and undue stress on joints can lead to OA in later life.
- A family history of OA is important as genetics plays a role in the causation of the disease.
- Faulty posture of the body during working or sitting may lead to OA of the spine of the back or neck.
- Aging itself is a cause of OA in many individuals who may not have any of the above causes.

How is OA treated

Treatment consists of hot and cold compresses, pain relief with medications prescribed by the physician, physical therapy, use of steroid drugs orally or injected into the joints, lifestyle management and occasionally surgical intervention. Replacement of the hip or the knee joint is a very common surgical treatment now a days and gives substantial benefit to the pain and movement of the joint. Various pain management techniques are also available for the treatment of OA.

What can you do to prevent OA in old age

The following are the important preventive strategies for the disease.

- Overweight and obesity are important in the causation of OA. Hence, maintaining a healthy body weight is one of the most important requisites to prevent OA in old age.
- Prevention of injury to joints is important in avoiding the disease in later life. Hence prevention of OA should begin in early age. Sports injuries and other injuries to the joint in young age may impair the function of the joint in later life and pave the way for development of OA. While exercising care should always be taken to warm up before the exercise and cool down during the last few minutes of the exercise. While doing stretches, the feet should always be kept flat on the floor. Twisting of the knees should be avoided and care taken to land on a bent knee while jumping. As far as possible, the elderly should take care to exercise on soft surfaces and avoid very hard surfaces like concrete floors. Proper sports shoes with the correct fit should be used while exercising. The elderly should be encouraged to perform brisk walking which is the best exercise for them and avoid very strenuous exercises like jogging or skipping. Swimming is a very pleasant and

acceptable exercise for the prevention of OA.

- Assuming proper ergonomic posture while walking, sitting, and lying down are important. Bad posture for prolonged periods is very important in causing OA. Improper posture can strain the spine and the muscles. A chronic bad posture places abnormal stress on the joints especially of the spine leading to OA in later life. Those working in the software industry should take special care to maintain proper posture while working. The furniture used also should be ergonomically acceptable. Working on the mobile phone for long periods and texting with the head bent is a cause of strain to the bones of the neck and muscles. This leads to pain and osteoarthritis of the spine. It is called 'Tech Syndrome' or 'Text Syndrome'. To avoid this the phone and computer should be kept at eye level and prolonged bent posture of the neck should be avoided. Frequent stretching of the neck should be done and every half an hour, the individual should take a five-minute break from the work that he is doing and stretch his muscles and change his body posture.
- Later in life exercising should be done carefully. Low impact exercises like walking, swimming, yoga, and tai chi may be performed and high impact exercises

like jogging should not be started in later life if the person is not already accustomed to it.

- Regular exercise from young age helps in keeping OA away from the joints as the person ages. Light aerobic exercises are advised according to the convenience and likes of the person. *Keeping physically active is the key word in the prevention of OA.*

- Any pain in the joints, if persisting for more than two or three days, should never be ignored and medical help should be sought.

- Proper nutrition with balanced nutrients is essential in the prevention of OA.

- Patients with other co-morbidities like diabetes should be very careful in regulating their blood sugar.

- It is very important to prevent falls in the elderly with OA, as falls are very common and can lead to disabling fractures.

- For the elderly patient who is already afflicted with the disease, adequate modifications will be needed in the home for independent living.

- The use of a cane or a walker will make the individual's life easier to move about and relieve joint pain by taking off the strain on the affected joints. Braces, custom shoes, and crutches also are available. Various other mobility assistive equipment are also available for these patients. Door knobs in the house may be replaced with handles.

- Easy grip utensils in the kitchen, key-turners, writing aids, the use of zippers instead of buttons in clothing are some of the modifications which can improve their quality of life (See section on *'Stroke'*)
- 'Smart-home' technologies are available for these modifications to make life easier for the arthritic patients.

RHEUMATOID ARTHRITIS

Rheumatoid arthritis (RA) is an autoimmune disease affecting the joints. *Autoimmunity* means that our immune system mistakenly attacks the normal cells and causes pain and swelling in these joints (*inflammation*). The disease attacks many joints together. It affects the lining of the joints which is called the *'synovial membrane'*. The joints of the hands, wrists, toes, and knees are often affected causing chronic pain and later causes deformity of the joints. The smaller joints of the body are affected first and later the larger joints like the shoulder and knee are affected. The disease when advanced, can also affect the eyes, heart, skin, or lungs.

As of 2021, almost 1.9 million people in the United States are afflicted with the disease. The disease is 3-4 times more common in women. The disease usually starts between the ages of 30 – 50 and is chronic and disabling by the time the person reaches old age. In about 10 – 33% the disease may start only in old age and is referred to as *Elderly onset Rheumatoid Arthritis.*

What are the symptoms of the disease

The disease often starts gradually with general symptoms like loss of appetite, mild fever, weight loss and generalized tiredness. *'Tired all the Time'* is a common complaint. Stiffness of joints especially of the fingers are one of the earliest symptoms that may occur. The stiffness of the joints is maximum when the patient wakes up in the morning and tends to decrease as the patient becomes active during the day. At night when the patient rests, the joints and the body do not move and remain in the same position for long periods. The joints, hence, tend to become stiff because of the same posture for a long time.

Other symptoms that the patient complains of are, inability to hold a spoon or ladle, inability to unscrew the cap of a bottle, difficulty in tying shoelaces, and buttoning and unbuttoning of clothes. Brushing teeth, turning a door knob, using the scissors, typing in a computer, pressing a TV remote control button, all become difficult tasks for them. Rings worn in the hand tend to get stuck at the finger joints which are swollen. Walking becomes difficult when the hip or knee joints are affected.

The joints are often swollen, red and painful. They may be warm to touch. Low grade fever may be present. Often the disease is symmetrical affecting the joints on both sides of the body. The movements of the joints are restricted. The patient's grip is weakened due to the muscle weakness and pain. Walking often causes a limp and loss of balance may occur.

When RA occurs in the elderly, it may progress rapidly and affect the larger joints more than the smaller ones. But it tends to be less severe than when it starts in the younger age group.

What complications can occur in RA

Complications of RA can affect various organs of the body.

- They may develop certain swellings called *Rheumatic nodules* at the joints of the fingers or elbows.
- The blood vessels of the skin may be affected to produce ulcer like spots on the skin.

- The white of the eye called the Sclera may show redness and pain.
- The lung may show scarring and there may be symptoms like wheezing due to the obstruction to the small airways in the lungs.
- Heart problems can develop in some patients.
- Thickening of the membrane (synovial) of the joints in the wrist can produce a condition called *'Carpel tunnel syndrome'* where the nerve supplying the palm which is in front of the wrist is compressed leading to pain and weakness of the thumb and some fingers.

What treatment is given for the disease.

It has to be stressed that the disease has no cure. Whatever treatment is offered is for suppressing pain and inflammation in the joints. Other measures are mainly for the rehabilitation of the patient and improving the quality of life.

Medications like steroids are given to reduce the inflammation of the joint. Other medications are given to modify the disease and reduce the chances of deformity occurring in the joint.

In addition to the medicines, self-management strategies and physical therapy are very important. Exercising the affected joints is needed to keep them flexible. One should take care to avoid exercising when the joint is painful. Intermittent breaks should be taken during the exercise periods and the exercises should not be too intense. The exercises should be done slowly. One should not exercise immediately on waking in the morning or just before going to bed. The patients should be encouraged to be physically active as much as possible and avoid a sedentary lifestyle.

Exercises like flexing and relaxing the fingers multiple times and making a fist, bending, and extending the toes and hip lift exercises may be performed. Walking is the simplest exercise for the larger joints of the lower limbs. A cane or walking-stick is helpful when walking. The help of a physical therapist may be sought.

In addition, hot fomentation helps to soothe the pain in the joints. When the joints are severely painful and inflamed, rest for the joints is essential and occasionally the limb may have to be splinted to prevent movement.

Management of stress is also important as stress can aggravate RA. Changes in the home environment may be needed as a warm environment may help some patients.

Adequate sleep is to be encouraged. Smoking is to be totally avoided.

Prevention of RA in the elderly

Altering the risk factors for a disease is the primary mode of preventing any disease. This holds good for RA also. However, there are risk factors for any disease some of which are Non-modifiable and others Modifiable. One should try to prevent the Modifiable risk factors.

The non-modifiable risk factors are Age, Family history and Gender. As we said earlier, women are more prone for the disease.

However, every effort should be made to avoid or change the modifiable risk factors of the disease.

- Stopping smoking is of paramount importance. The patient should also avoid exposure to passive smoke.
- Losing weight is an important preventive measure. The help of a dietician and physical therapist should be sought whenever needed.

- Avoiding exposure to environmental pollution is also important in the prevention of RA.
- Regular exercise in younger age carried into old age is highly recommended for preventing all types of arthritis in old age. Regular aerobic exercises like walking, swimming, and biking are ideal and must be done at least for half hour daily five or six times a week. Strength exercises like the elastic bands or resistance exercises with mild weights may be done two or three times a week to improve the strength of the muscles. Stretching exercises also are important. Yoga, Tai-chi, and other similar exercises are also worth exploring.
- Avoiding injury to the joints is also important (See section on *Osteoarthritis*).
- While working and at home, ergonomic measures should be tried to prevent strain on the joints and muscles. Keep your computer about 15 -20 degrees below eye level to avoid straining your neck. Use an ergonomic keyboard and mouse. The chair should have a lumbar support and preferably a headrest also. Use a cushion to support the small of the back while sitting. Sit upright with the spine erect. Place your feet on the floor or on a simple foot rest. While working in the office for long periods, take a break frequently and just walk around and stretch your arms and

neck for a couple of minutes before resuming work.

- Avoid infections. Respiratory infections like cold and flu may trigger exacerbations of RA. Avoid crowded places. The elderly should compulsorily have their Flu shots, Covid and pneumonia vaccinations taken. It is preferable to wear face masks in crowded places.
- Don't ignore any symptoms. Even minor symptoms in the joints, if persistent for more than three or four days need urgent medical attention.

OSTEOPOROSIS

Osteoporosis (**OP**) is another common bone disorder seen in the elderly. As the name implies, the bone becomes more 'porous' or loses its density and becomes brittle. WHO defined osteoporosis as ' *a systemic skeletal disease characterized by low bone mass, leading to increased bone fragility and fractures'*.

Osteoporosis can occur due to various causes.

In 5 – 20% of women OP can occur within 15-20 years of menopause and is called *Post-Menopausal Osteoporosis.*

In both men and women older than 70 years, OP can occur leading to fragility and increased chances of fractures of hip, spine, and long bones. This is called *Senile Osteoporosis.*

Occasionally various diseases like Hormone imbalances, cancer, digestive problems, side effects of medications, kidney diseases, poor nutrition, or prolonged bed rest due to any illness can all lead to Osteoporosis. This is called *Secondary Osteoporosis.*

Estimates put the global burden of OP at around 200 million individuals. After the age of fifty, 1 out of 2 women and 1 out of 4 men may develop OP related fractures at some time in their lifetime. OP causes approximately 9 million fractures annually in the world. Of this 1.6 million are fractures of the hip, 1.4 million are fractures of the vertebrae and 1.7 million are forearm fractures. Europe and North America together account for 51% of the total number of the world's osteoporosis fractures. In the US it is estimated that around 61 million men and women over the age of 50 have OP.

What are the Risk factors for Osteoporosis

Various risk factors contribute to the development of OP in old age.

- A genetic predisposition to develop OP exists in almost 70% of patients.
- Non-Modifiable Risk Factors are as follows.
  o Age, Gender, and Ethnicity are important. Those over 60 are more prone to OP.
  o Females have greater propensity to develop OP.
  o Caucasians and Asians are at an increased risk of developing OP compared to Hispanics and Afro-Americans since they have a higher bone mass genetically and hence are generally protected against OP.
- Modifiable Risk Factors are equally important.
  o Early menopause.
  o Surgical removal of ovaries.
  o Low testosterone (male hormone) levels in males.
  o Malnutrition.
  o Inadequate intake of Calcium and Vitamin D.
  o Use of steroids for prolonged periods as is given for certain diseases.

- Sedentary life with very low physical activity.
- Heavy alcohol intake.
- Smoking. Females who smoke have a higher chance of developing osteoporosis.
- Abuse of elders and neglect are also risk factors which have to be taken into consideration. Physical abuse and neglect leading to poor nutrition, falls and fractures should also be considered.

What are the symptoms of the disease

Osteoporosis is a disease which produces no symptoms till a fracture occurs. It may be routinely detected in patients when a test for bone mineral density is performed by the physician. A fracture may be the first indication that OP exists.

Even a minor trauma may be sufficient to cause a fracture. Tripping on a rug while walking in the home may lead to a fall leading to fracture hip of bones of the thigh. Repeated fractures are also common in this disease. This leads to increased morbidity and mortality.

Hip fractures are the most significant. 15-30% of patients may die during the first six months after a hip fracture and 1 out of 5 die during the first year. This is mainly due to the decrease in mobility, surgery, and being bedridden. Approximately 3,50,000 Americans are treated with hip fractures every year. Of these 90% are due to falls.

Vertebral fractures increase the morbidity. They cause back pain, deformity of the spine leading to a *'Hunch back'* or a *'Dowager's Hump'*, decrease in the size of the chest wall which in turn causes the lung to be restricted leading to breathing difficulties.

Wrist fractures are often caused when the patient falls on an outstretched hand. Generally, patients with osteoporosis are more likely to fall than others of the same age.

The disease is diagnosed by X-rays of the spine and other long bones. A test to assess the density of the bone called *'Bone Densitometry'* or Osteoporosis Scan is available to detect osteoporosis.

Treatment is mainly preventive. There are medications which to some extent improve the bone density and may be given. Replacement of female hormones to women (*Hormone Replacement Therapy*) is also given to some.

How can we prevent Osteoporosis from developing in old age

A balanced diet with adequate nutrients, adequate intake of Vitamin D and calcium from foods like yoghurt, cheese, milk, nuts, and green leafy vegetables should be encouraged.

- Heavy intake of alcohol to be avoided.
- Smoking should be totally avoided.
- Exercise: Teenagers should be encouraged to exercise regularly to build bone mass and this should be continued into adulthood. The elderly should be encouraged to exercise depending on their physical capacity. Simple aerobic exercises are sufficient. Once or twice a week, resistance exercises like mild weight lifting or exercise bands are helpful in building bone strength.
- All precautions should be taken to prevent falls in the elderly. (*See Section on 'Falls in the Elderly'*)

Resources

1. Davidson's Principles and Practice of Medicine. 23rd Edition, Elsevier 2018 Chapter 24, 981 – 1060.
2. Osteoarthritis (OA) Center for Disease Control and Prevention.
3. A National Public Health Agenda for Osteoarthritis. 2020 Update.
4. Everything you need to know about Osteoarthritis. Henry Ford Health. 2021.

5. Rheumatoid Arthritis (RA) Center for Disease Control and Prevention.
6. Arthritis Patient Care. Center for Disease Control and Prevention.
7. Osteoporosis. National Institute on Aging.
8. Osteoporosis Overview. National Institute of Arthritis and Musculoskeletal and Skin Diseases.

Chapter 7. EAR, NOSE & THROAT

Structure & Function. *The Ear, Nose and Throat form one single unit even though they are different parts of the body.*

The Ear: *The ear has three parts called the External Ear, Middle Ear, and the Inner Ear. The external ear is the hearing structure that you see on the sides of the head. It is made of cartilage. It leads into a one-inch canal called the ear canal. The canal ends in a thin membrane called the* **Tympanic Membrane** *or the Ear Drum. Beyond the ear drum lies a cavity called the Middle ear. This is filled with air and contains three tiny bones called 'ossicles' which are connected to each other. The ossicles connect to the inner ear which is inside the bone of the skull and contains the hearing and balancing apparatus of the ear. The hearing apparatus is a small, coiled snail-like structure called 'Cochlea'. In addition, there are three tubes or canals called 'Semi-circular canals' situated at right angles to each other filled with fluid which helps us to maintain the balance of our body. The inner ear has fine nerves which convey the hearing signals to the brain.* **(See Fig. 9***)*

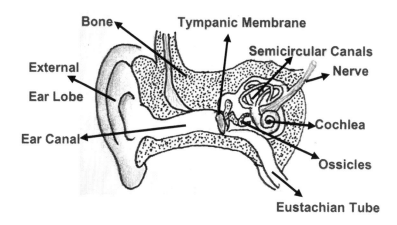

Figure 9. (Ear – Structure)

When we receive sound with the external ear, it enters the ear canal and strikes the ear drum (tympanic membrane). The ear drum vibrates and these vibrations are transmitted through the three tiny ossicles to the inner ear. These vibrations are converted to signals by the nerves in the inner ear and are transmitted to the brain to be recognized and interpreted. A thin tube called **Eustachian Tube** connects the middle ear to the throat. This tube helps to drain fluid from the middle ear and equalize the air pressure inside the ear.

The semicircular canals are also connected to the nerves in the inner ear and help maintain the body's balance.

The Nose : The nose is the first organ of the respiratory system. It is formed of two nostrils on either side separated by a flat cartilage in the center. Air enters the nose through the nostrils and is filtered at the entry by fine hairs present in the nostrils. The nose is also the organ of smell. Inside the cavity of the nose, in its roof there are fine nerves which pick up the sensations of smell and transmit them to the brain. The nose is also important in speech as the many air-filled sinuses *which surround the nose act as resonating columns and help in modulating one's voice.*

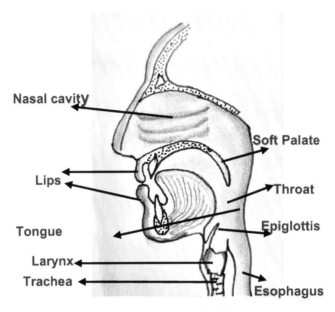

Figure 10 (Nose & Throat)

The Throat : The throat consist of two part called the **Pharynx** and the **Larynx**. It is like the traffic junction of the respiratory and the digestive system. The pharynx is the space at the back of the mouth. It is connected above to the nose. Below there are two structures, the voice box or larynx in front and the food tube or the gullet also called the esophagus behind it. The esophagus carries the food to the stomach. The larynx continues down as the trachea (wind pipe) which is the tube that conveys air to the lungs. (**See fig. 10**)

There is a small, flat flap-like fold of cartilage above the larynx. It is called the **epiglottis** and prevents food and liquids from entering the larynx when we swallow.

Aging produces many senile changes associated with the ear, nose, and throat. It is found that over 15% of the elderly over 65 years are frail and have problems connected with the ear, nose, or throat. Many elderly individuals find it difficult to communicate with their peers or loved ones. These may be due to the natural process of aging causing hearing loss, changes in voice, acid reflux from the stomach, and swallowing problems which can impair speech. In this section, we shall, in brief discuss what problems the elderly face due to these.

HEARING LOSS

The hearing loss of the elderly is called **Presbycusis** in medical parlance. It is a progressive, irreversible, and symmetrical decrease in hearing that occurs in both the ears. It is due to the damage to the nerves involved in hearing. As per the WHO hearing loss is the second most common geriatric illness. The National Institute of Aging reports that one out of three patients over 65 and half of those above 75 years have some amount of hearing loss. This is seen more commonly in men and can lead to falls, accidents, and depression in the individual. The loss is mainly for the high frequency sounds. Hearing loss affects around 30 million people in the US each year.

This hearing loss in the elderly is accentuated when the noise in the surroundings is more e.g., in shopping malls, busy streets, bus and railway stations, restaurants, bazaars etc. At home, loud music or the TV may interfere with hearing in them. The elderly individual may often be unaware of this disability and hence tend to speak louder than normal. High pitched sounds like ringing bells, whistles, music from flutes, a child's high-pitched squeal or voice, may not be heard properly by them.

The damage to hearing can also follow the exposure to very high noise as in factories or stone quarries where the noise is very loud and unless, the person has been wearing protective ear muffs, this can lead to hearing loss in later life.

Other factors that can affect hearing loss are smoking, diseases like high blood pressure or diabetes, heavy metal exposure, certain medications like Aspirin, some antibiotics and medicines given for heart failure, and some hormonal factors.

What are the consequences of Age-Related Hearing Loss

Age Related Hearing Loss **(ARHL)** can be very much incapacitating for the elderly individual who already may be affected by other co-existing illnesses. Hearing loss may go unrecognized in early stages. And often it is the spouse who notices this defect for the first time. Some of the adverse effects of this disability are as follows.

- ARHL is a risk factor in the development of dementia as cognitive functions may decline faster in individuals with hearing impairment. . It is reported that dementia is 2 – 4 times more in these patients. Proper treatment of this condition can mitigate the effects of dementia to some extent.
- Often the person hears voices which are distorted and not necessarily muffled as they may not hear certain tones and frequencies and hence cannot grasp what is being said. High pitched sounds like 's' 'th' 'f' 't' or 'p' are not recognized properly. The person can hear a man's voice better than a woman's due to the higher pitch of the latter. They often have trouble talking on the phone.
- The person feels that others are 'mumbling' and not speaking clearly. They frequently ask the other person to repeat what they

said. They find it difficult to hear women and children speaking.

- Some patients may feel a 'ringing' or 'buzzing' or 'hissing' sound in the ear. It is called *tinnitus* and is often an annoying symptom.
- The quality of life of the individual is reduced as it may lead to depression, social isolation, and loneliness.
- Those who are still working may find that their productivity is reduced and their interpersonal relationships in the organization also suffers.
- Falls are twice more common when the hearing is impaired. Often balance is also affected along with the hearing loss and the person may feel unsteady while standing or walking. In addition, the individual may not heed warnings or vehicle sounds or horns making them prone to accidents. There is a general lack of environmental awareness in these individuals.

Any doubt regarding the hearing of an elderly individual should be promptly brought to the attention of the doctor and appropriate treatment instituted at the earliest. Early treatment of the condition to a large extent prevents progression of hearing loss.

ARHL is diagnosed using a test called *Audiometry* which is performed by the technician. This tests the intensity and the tone of sounds heard. The ability to hear different sounds, pitches and frequencies are tested. It is a simple test for hearing function. In addition, tests like Word recognition and Speech recognition are also tested.

The treatment is mainly provided by the ENT specialist doctor who is called an *Otorhinolaryngologist* (quite a mouthful!). Technological advancements have now made very advanced and wireless hearing aids available for the treatment of hearing loss. These hearing aids can also be synchronized with smart phones, TV, Music systems and Internet of Things to interact with appliances in the home of the patient like smoke detectors, door bells, alarm systems etc.

Implantable devices are also now available which can aid hearing. The doctor will often be able to advice the patient on the appropriate hearing aid depending on the requirements of the person.

What should an elderly person with ARHL do

- They should be careful to let others know that they have a hearing impairment. There is no need to be ashamed of this.
- They should request people to face them when they speak.

- They should ask people to repeat what they said, if they do not understand what was said.
- They should avoid crowded places to talk with others. A comparatively quiet place should be chosen for conversation.
- An opinion from an ENT surgeon as to how best they can be treated should be obtained. If the doctor prescribes a hearing aid, one should be familiar with its use.

How to communicate with an elderly person with ARHL

Here are some tips for the caregiver or relative to communicate with an elderly loved one with hearing loss.

- As far as possible, one should stand in front of them and draw their attention before speaking to them. They may be gently tapped on their shoulder to get their attention.
- Background noise must be reduced. Other people talking loudly, TV or radio blaring, music system playing, or gatherings like a marriage reception, a busy bazaar, railway, and bus stations are places where their hearing impairment becomes aggravated. One should move to a quieter place, if possible to speak to them.

- Always speak clearly, slowly, and loudly. One should not shout or mumble while talking to them.
- When in a group only one person should speak to them at a time.
- If needed, one should repeat oneself if they do not properly hear what was said. One should be patient with those with hearing impairment.
- If they don't grasp what was said, it has to be rephrased in a different manner.
- When speaking to them, make eye contact. Talk to them in a place with adequate lighting and use gestures when needed. Be sympathetic and caring.
- Do not talk to them from another room or from a distance, or when you are facing away from them.
- It is better to address the person by name or by relationship like Mr. Smith, Daddy or Mummy when speaking to them.
- Don't cover your face or mouth when speaking. Beards and moustaches of the speaker can pose a problem to some patients.
- When the person with hearing impairment is speaking, do not interrupt them.

- When a need to give instructions to them arises, use a written text or directions with a diagram.
- When in a group, always include them in the conversation. This prevents social isolation in them and a feeling of depression. Do not ignore them. Keep them in the loop whenever possible.

VOICE CHANGES

Only humans have the ability to speak and communicate with each other using their voices though it is known that animals and birds too communicate with each other with sounds. Speech needs a coordinated effort of the respiratory and nervous system to produce the voice. In addition, the muscles of the voice box in the neck also act to generate a person's voice. The change in the voice which occur in old age is called **_Presbyphonia_**.

As a person grows old, natural changes occur in one's voice which can have an impact on the social and professional life of an individual. This is because the small joints in the voice box (Larynx) become stiffer and calcium may be deposited in the voice box. The muscles of the larynx concerned with speech also become thinner and weaker.

Approximately, 10% of individuals develop voice changes as age advances.

What are the changes that occur in the voice with aging

- The loudness of the voice tends to decrease as age advances.
- As the person continues to speak, his voice tends to become feebler and fade away. This is called *Voice Fatigue.*
- An alteration in the pitch of the voice may occur with age. Men may develop a higher pitch and women, a lower pitch.
- A tremor or shakiness of the voice may develop in some individuals.
- The voice may become rough or breathy in some individuals.
- In addition to this, diseases affecting the respiratory system like Asthma, Allergy or Chronic Obstructive Pulmonary Disease can also weaken and affect the voice in the elderly.

Singers are affected the most. Singing makes one's voice stable and gives the person the ability to increase phonation to the maximum. This tends to decrease with age. However, constant practice can still help maintain the singer's voice well into old age.

There are treatments available to benefit the patient whose voice changes with age. Training with the aid of a speech therapist will help rehabilitating the patient. The tremor in the voice may be relieved with injection of *Botulinum toxin* (Botox) locally into the voice box. Local injections into the vocal cord to thicken them are used in some patients. The patients may have to undergo surgery with implants in some cases to restore their voice.

How can you keep your voice healthy in old age

There are many ways in which one can prevent changes in the voice with old age.

- Vocal hygiene is important. One should drink at least 6 – 8 glasses of water daily to keep oneself well hydrated. Speaking very loudly and shouting should be avoided. One should not speak when the voice is hoarse or when one's voice is tired. Give the voice some rest.
- Noisy environments where one may have to raise the voice to speak should be avoided.
- Minimum consumption of caffeinated beverages and alcohol is preferable.
- Smoking and exposure to environmental smoke, dust, or other irritant gases in one's surroundings should be avoided. A face mask should be worn when cleaning or dusting in the home.
- A humidifier will be useful in winter and in very dry climatic conditions. A 30% humidity is ideal.

- Spicy foods are better avoided. These can cause acid reflux from the stomach into the throat and affect one's voice. Troublesome heartburn needs to be treated by a physician.
- Consumption of good nourishing food and adequate exercise are recommended. Exercise increases one's overall muscle strength and improves breathing by strengthening the muscles of the respiratory system.
- Mouthwashes or gargles that have irritating chemicals or alcohol should not be used.
- Overuse of one's voice should be avoided. Shouting and screaming are harmful. Whispering also causes strain on the voice.
- One should keep away from patients who have a cold, cough, or other respiratory infections.
- Training one's voice by reading aloud for 20-30 minutes daily is helpful in keeping the voice healthy. Reading from a book or the newspaper loudly for half an hour daily must be made a regular habit. Singing whenever possible is another way to keep one's voice healthy in old age. Storytelling to the grand kids is a promising way to a healthy voice and sociability. Not using the voice with prolonged periods of silence can also lead to problems. Humming into a straw has been advocated as one method of training the voice in old age.

SWALLOWING

Difficulty is swallowing is called **Dysphagia** in medical parlance. Swallowing difficulties occur in 37 to 78% of the elderly who are affected with stroke, Parkinson's disease, or Alzheimer's disease. In those who have no obvious disease affecting the nervous system, it is still seen in 10-33% of elderly individuals. Approximately 6 million elderly individuals in the US have difficulty in swallowing. This can later lead to other problems like malnutrition, pneumonia, or dehydration.

What are the changes which occur with aging

The difficulty in swallowing which accompanies old age is called **Presbyphagia**. Swallowing normally is a combination of voluntary and involuntary muscles in and around the mouth and throat and is a complicated process. As a person ages, the muscles in the tongue tend to become weak and smaller. Further, the dryness of the mouth which occurs with old age makes swallowing more difficult. Other associated conditions like diabetes, dementia and other diseases also may affect the process of swallowing. There are some medications too that can affect swallowing. Poor oral hygiene and lack of teeth can also impede the swallowing process.

The first phase of swallowing is voluntary where the individual chews the food and swallows it. After this, the swallowing process becomes involuntary.

Elderly individuals may have difficulty in swallowing solids only, liquids only or both. The concern regarding swallowing is important as this can subsequently lead to poor nutrition, dehydration, inability to take medications, weight loss or aspiration of the contents into the windpipe leading to choking and pneumonia.

What are the causes of swallowing difficulties in the elderly

There are many causes for the difficulties that the elderly may face during swallowing.

- Poor oral hygiene and poor condition of the teeth may be a cause of inability to chew and swallow. Ill-fitting dentures could make swallowing difficult.
- Weakening of the muscles of the throat may cause swallowing problems. The tongue becomes smaller and weaker as age advances.

- Acid reflux which occurs in some individuals may lead to difficulty in swallowing.
- Certain medications may cause difficulty in swallowing.
- Cancer of the mouth, throat or food pipe may be a cause of swallowing difficulties.

What symptoms does the patient have

- Sudden coughing while eating or drinking may be a common feature of swallowing problems in old age.
- They may choke on solids, liquids or when trying to swallow tablets and feel that the food 'went the wrong way'. They feel that food or tablets get "stuck" in their throat.
- Sometimes the food they swallow may be regurgitated immediately.
- The person may experience a change in voice after eating or drinking.
- The person may feel that his food is being stuck in his chest behind the breastbone after swallowing and he has to drink water or other liquids to get it down.
- In severe cases, the patient may not be able to swallow the saliva produced in his mouth leading to drooling of saliva. This is seen in severe obstructions in the throat or food pipe like cancers.
- Recent loss of weight, repeated infections in the chest and a feeling of burning in the chest may be experienced by some.

How can we help a patient with swallowing difficulties.

Conditions where the patients are suffering from a disease like cancer, stroke, muscular weakness, or Alzheimer's disease which is causing the swallowing problem need professional help from a doctor or other medical services. We shall be dealing only with those persons who routinely feel some difficulty in swallowing because of the old age. Some of the simple measures that can help these persons are as follows:

- Some elderly individuals are unable to swallow their tablets with water. In such cases, the tablets must be crushed and administered with a thick beverage like gruel or mixed with food. Or they can be given with vanilla or chocolate pudding, honey, or apple sauce to mask the bad taste of the crushed tablet and given to the patient for easy swallowing. (See below on *How to swallow a tablet*).

- The elderly person should be advised to chew his food fully and properly before swallowing. When eating dry foods like bread or biscuits, the person should be encouraged to take some liquid along with it. Cookies or rusks may be dipped in coffee or tea and taken to soften them and ease swallowing.

- Some elderly people may not be able to drink fluids using straws as it may give them a sudden choking feeling. This should be avoided.
- Elderly people should take precautions to be adequately hydrated to prevent a dry mouth. Some find it difficult to drink plain water. In them, water may be mixed with a thickening agent or they may be given a fruit juice which could be easily swallowed.
- The person should be given adequate nutrition in the form of high fat foods like yoghurt, soft cheeses, coconut cream, avocado or peanut butter which may be added to tasty dishes.
- Easily pureed foods like squashed foods, steamed vegetables, fruits which are ripe and soft may be given. They can be mixed with soups or pureed and given to the person. Protein powder may also be added to augment protein intake.
- Milk can be made into smoothies, blended with banana, squash or butter to make it thicker and easier to swallow.
- The person should always be sitting upright when eating or drinking. Do not allow them to eat or drink in the semi recumbent or lying posture.
- If they find it difficult to swallow, they get tired of eating. Hence, meals may be given in small portions frequently, say, every two

or three hourly to keep them well nourished.

How to swallow a tablet.

- o First of all, drink a little water to wet your throat.
- o Next, place the tablet in your mouth and take half a mouthful of water.
- o Tilt your head backwards so that the tablet reaches the back of your tongue along with the water.
- o Press the tip of your tongue to the roof of the mouth in the front and tilt your head slightly forward.
- o In this position, swallow the tablet. It will pass smoothly into the throat without getting stuck.

DIZZINESS AND VERTIGO

Vertigo and dizziness are common symptoms in the elderly. Vertigo means a feeling of whirling or spinning with loss of balance due to disease of the inner part of the ear. Dizziness is a feeling of fainting, lightheadedness, or unsteadiness of the body. In the elderly it is a common symptom seen in 10-35% of individuals. It is more common after the age of 80 (50%). Often this is a cause of falls in the elderly.

- Dizziness can occur due to a variety of reasons.
- Diseases of the Nervous system can cause dizziness.
- Any problem with vision can lead to dizziness.
- Some psychological problems like anxiety and depression can lead to dizziness.
- Other metabolic changes in the body can lead to dizziness e.g., Anemia, Fever, Dehydration, decrease in sodium in the blood etc.
- Medications of various types can lead to dizziness. Medicines taken for heart disease, diseases of the brain and nervous system, sedatives, allergy medications, psychiatric medications are some of them which cause dizziness.

Vertigo on the other hand is due to diseases affecting the innermost part of the ear which is concerned with maintaining the balance of the individual. The patient feels a sense of whirling as if he is spinning on a wheel and tends to lose his balance and fall.

The commonest cause is called *Benign Paroxysmal Positional Vertigo* (BPPV) which indicates an affliction of the balancing mechanism in the inner part of the ear. Sudden change in the position of the head like lying down, sitting up or turning over in bed, leads to vertigo and this may cause the patient to fall. It lasts for a minute or so and disappears only to recur again later. These episodes can occur frequently and be annoying at the same time dangerous as they may lead to falls and injury. Occasionally there may be nausea or vomiting along with vertigo.

There are other diseases like inflammation of the inner ear and decrease in blood flow to the inner ear which can lead to vertigo and dizziness.

The doctor treats the vertigo with certain medications which gives temporary relief. There are certain maneuvers which the ENT doctor performs keeping the head in different positions which helps to reduce the vertigo. Some exercises are also advised for the patient.

What can we do to prevent dizziness and vertigo in old age

- One should keep oneself well hydrated by drinking enough water.
- Vitamin C, D and E are said to be helpful. These are available in fruits and vegetables and hence their consumption is important.
- The elderly should be encouraged to walk with the help of a cane or walker to prevent sudden falls on feeling giddy.

- Avoid caffeine, alcohol, tobacco, or excess salt in diet.
- Any problem with vision should be corrected. This includes wearing corrective glasses and surgery for cataract. It is to be noted that some elders who wear bifocal lenses find it difficult to adjust to the glasses. Hence bifocal lenses should be substituted by separate reading glasses for them. Bifocal lenses should especially be avoided when using the stairs.
- Regular exercise like walking help to keep up the muscle tone and maintain balance. Balance exercises as advised by the physical therapist also can be undertaken. Yoga and Tai-Chi are exercises which help to improve strength and balance in the elderly individuals.
- Fever, vomiting, weakness, severe headache, or loss of consciousness should be brought to the attention of the doctor immediately and appropriate treatment given.
- Using proper foot wear, home modifications, installation of grab rails in the bathrooms are other precautionary measures which should be adopted.

LARYGOPHARYNGEAL REFLUX

Laryngopharyngeal Reflux (**LPR**) is a condition where the acid that is present in the stomach travels up into the food pipe (***Esophagus***) and surges back into the throat causing problems. It causes irritation in the throat and in the larynx (voice box). The elderly are more prone to develop this condition as LPR increases with age. One-third of people over the age of 75 have some sort of such reflux disease. This is because the ring-like muscle which tightly closes the lower end of the food pipe becomes lax and permits contents of the stomach to flow back into the throat. Weakness of the muscles in the food pipe, and certain medications which the patient may be taking may cause this. People with certain dietary habits like overeating, consuming highly spicy food or drinking alcohol are prone to this disease. Stress and overweight also contribute to the reflux.

What are the symptoms of LPR

The symptoms of LPR are felt in the throat and occasionally behind the breast bone in the chest.

- Soreness in the throat and a feeling of lump in the throat.
- Hoarseness of voice. Occasionally the person gets a hacking cough. The cough may be precipitated on lying down especially after food.
- A sensation of something sticking in the throat and having to clear one's throat often.
- Difficulty in swallowing.
- Frequent belching, heartburn.

Prevention of Laryngopharyngeal Reflux

Some of the measures to prevent this malady are as follows:

- Avoid smoking, alcohol, and excess caffeine.
- Reducing weight in overweight persons.
- Avoiding foods like chocolates, fatty foods, citrus fruits, carbonated beverages, mint flavored foods, red wine, and spicy foods.
- Avoiding tight clothing or a tight belt around the waist.
- Taking meals two or three hours before bedtime is an important measure to prevent LPR on lying down.
- Avoid lying down immediately after eating or drinking anything.

- Eating three or four times a day and limiting the quantity of food taken at each meal.
- Raising the head end of the bed will be helpful in some individuals. Any fluid or food should always be taken sitting up. Do not allow the person to eat or drink while lying down.

Treatment is mainly by modifying the lifestyle as mentioned above. In addition, the doctor may prescribe medications like Proton pump inhibitors that block excessive acid in the stomach. Antacids also are useful. Losing weight and going to bed at least two hours after meals is important. In rare cases, surgery may be needed to correct the intractable symptoms of LPR.

MISCELLANEOUS PROBLEMS

There are other minor problems which may trouble the elderly individuals and a brief account is given below.

Rhinitis

Rhinitis means inflammation of the nasal passages or simply a running nose or a stuffy nose as occurs during a common cold. It is common in the elderly but often ignored or unrecognized in them. They may have runny nose, post nasal drip, nasal stuffiness, sneezing, nasal dryness or crusting in the nostrils. The nasal stuffiness is more when they lie down. There may be a constant cough and bringing up of sputum. They may have to clear their throat very often. Long standing symptoms may lead to decrease in smell and taste.

The causes for the condition may be many. Allergies, dust, environmental conditions, medicines being taken by the patient may all cause rhinitis. Medications given for high blood pressure, psychiatric medicines and some pain killers may cause rhinitis.

Treatment is mainly prescribed by the ENT specialist and consists of medicines which may relieve the nasal congestion along with nasal sprays or drops. The individual should have a humidifier in his room. Steam inhalation is helpful in humidifying the nasal passages.

Taste and Smell

Taste and smell decline with age and can affect the safety, food intake and the quality of life of the elderly individuals. About 50% of persons in the age group 65-80, have some loss of smell. Above the age of 80, 75% of individuals may have loss of smell. Covid-19 is a recent illness which can produce loss of taste and smell in a person.

Smell is a safety precaution in us. The dangers of this loss of smell and taste may be that the person does not recognize spoilt food, fails to detect a gas leak or smoke in the home, or the smell of chemicals and detergents like petrol or kerosene. This can pose a danger to the health and life of the person.

The causes of loss or taste in an elderly person can be due to malnutrition, some medications, poor dental hygiene, or faulty dentures.

Exposure to air pollution, cigarette smoke, and infections can cause loss of smell in an individual. Diseases like Alzheimer's disease and Parkinson's disease can also decrease the sense of smell.

Recognition of these abnormalities is of paramount importance in instructing these individuals about the hazards that they may face and informing them to take adequate precautions.

Resources.

1. How to communicate with hearing impaired loved ones. Aging Care.com 2021

2. Hearing Loss – John Hopkins Medicine (Health)
3. Is loss of taste and smell normal with aging – Healthy Aging – Mayo Clinic.
4. Smell and Taste Disorders. John Hopkins Medicine

5. Taking care of your voice. National Institute of Deafness and other Communication Disorders.
6. Understanding voice disorders in seniors – Parentgiving.com
7. Mayo Clinic Proceedings Vol 96 issue 2. Feb 2021 pages 488-497
8. Aging and Swallowing-ENT Health – American Academy of Otolaryngology – Head and neck surgery.
9. Tips for seniors and caregivers managing dysphagia – Daily Caring
10. Choking on water. Why do elderly adults have difficulty swallowing.
11.Vertigo and dizziness in the Elderly. – Frontiers in Neurology
12.Dizziness – Cleveland Clinic.
13.Laryngopharyngeal Reflux – National Library of Medicine
14.Diagnosis and management of Laryngopharyngeal Reflux -American Family Physician
15.GERD and LPR – ENT Health
16.Geriatric Rhinitis – ENT Health

17. Rhinitis in the Elderly. National Library of Medicine
18.   Otolaryngologic Clinics of North America : Supp. Geriatric Otolaryngology. Ed. Mirza. N, Lee. JY. Aug 2018. Vol 51. Number 4

Chapter 8. NUTRITIONAL REQUIREMENTS

Knowing is not enough, we must apply

Willing is not enough, we must do. –
Goethe

As age advances, the ability for independent living and performing daily tasks become difficult due to various reasons. It is in this context that nutrition becomes a challenging and an important element of the elderly individuals. Many factors contribute to compromising the nutritional status of these individuals leading to ***Malnutrition.***

Malnutrition refers to deficiencies, excesses, or imbalances in a person's intake of energy and/or nutrients (WHO). It can be either undernutrition with loss of weight or deficiency of nutrients or overweight or obesity where excess calories are consumed. The poor nutritional status in turn leads to other problems like increased susceptibility to infections and even death. '*An unintended loss of body mass (> 5 % in six months or > 10 % beyond six months) or a markedly reduced body mass index (i.e., BMI <20 kg/m²) or muscle mass should be regarded as serious signs of malnutrition*'. (ESPEN Guidelines). Hence, **Dehydration** and **Obesity** are also considered nutritional problems in the elderly population.

NUTRITION

What are the causes for Nutritional Deficiencies in the Elderly

Multiple factors contribute to the occurrence of nutritional deficiencies in elderly individuals. Some of them are outlined below.

- Living alone, going shopping and cooking become cumbersome as age advances and the individual tends to cut down on food owing to this.

- Poor health due to co-existing disease conditions may impair tasks like cooking and feeding oneself. Arthritis of the joints of the hand may make cooking and eating a difficult task.
- Medications being taken by the person may change the taste of the food or decrease appetite. Some medications cause nausea and vomiting.
- As age advances the sense of taste and smell decrease and the person may not be able to appreciate the taste and smell of food leading to lesser food intake. The inability to differentiate stale food from fresh food may be detrimental to their health.
- Loss of teeth, poor dentition, ill-fitting dentures, poor oral hygiene, and the difficulty to chew due to muscle weakness may all be causative factors.
- Swallowing may become a problem due to weakness of the muscles of the throat.
- Depression and loneliness in the individual may make them apathetic and hence they may avoid eating and skip meals.
- Memory loss renders them forgetful to buy food and store them. Some forget whether they had their meals or not.
- Financial problems may lead to the purchase of cheap foods and those which are less nutritious. Further, transportation problems and adverse climate make them

unable to go shopping which leads to poor feeding and consequent malnutrition.

How much nutrition does an elderly need?

The nutritional needs of an individual changes as he ages. The elderly generally require about 20% lesser calories than and adult of the same weight and height. The reasons for this are their less active lifestyle, poor digestive function, dental problems, swallowing difficulties and other co-existing illnesses. The estimated calorie needs of elderly individuals above the age of 61 have been listed below. (*Dietary Guidelines for Americans 2020-2025*).

Gender	Sedentary	Mod. Active	Active
Men	2000	2400	2600
Women	1600	1800	2000

a) Sedentary means a lifestyle that includes only the physical activity of independent living.

b) Moderately Active means a lifestyle that includes physical activity equivalent to walking about 1.5 to 3 miles per day at 3 to 4 miles per hour, in addition to the activities of independent living.

c) Active means a lifestyle that includes physical activity equivalent to walking more than 3 miles per day at 3 to 4 miles per hour, in addition to the activities of independent living.

[Source: Institute of Medicine. Dietary Reference Intakes for Energy, Carbohydrate, Fiber, Fat, Fatty Acids,

Cholesterol, Protein, and Amino Acids. Washington (DC): The National Academies Press; 2002.]

Older persons need fewer number of calories. Excess calories leads to obesity especially when their activities are restricted. Even though the caloric needs decrease, their nutritional needs of vitamins and minerals may remain normal or even increase slightly.

How to eat healthy as you grow old

Nutrition is important at all ages of an individual, but special importance must be given to the nutrition of the elderly as their need for calories may not be high but the need for essential nutrients is higher than for a normal adult. Hence special attention is needed in their daily food intake. Some principles of healthy eating as one grows old are discussed below.

- As age advances, one should take care to avoid the 'Empty Calories' as are present in aerated drinks, soda, alcohol, chips, candies, and baked goods.
- More foods low in fat and cholesterol should be included in the diet. As far as possible, avoid saturated fats like butter, margarine, *ghee*, and trans fats like margarine, vegetable shortening, oil reused

after frying (used in some fast-food outlets).

- Eating nutrients, at the same time, not increasing the caloric intake is important. To achieve this more fruits and vegetables should be consumed. There should be at least 3 – 5 portions of fruits and vegetables in their daily diet. Whole grains, whole wheat, brown rice, pulses, cereals, and oatmeal are preferred choices. Sea food and lean meat provide nutrients and proteins. Vegetarians should take beans, nuts, seeds, and legumes. Low fat milk fortified with Vitamin D and Calcium is an ideal food.

- Adequate fluid intake in the form of juices or water should be ensured in the elderly as they can easily become dehydrated due to many reasons. The elderly individual has a decreased sense of thirst, and this can lead to poor intake of fluids. Others may purposely avoid drinking fluids as they may have problems with their bladder like urinary incontinence and to avoid passing urine frequently, they voluntarily reduce their fluid intake. At least 8 glasses of fluid / water intake should be ensured per day. The elderly person may not feel thirsty and may feel reluctant to walk to the kitchen or to the water dispenser. It should be noted that the color of the urine in them should be light and not dark due to the concentration of urine. Restriction of fluid intake may be advised by the doctor in those with diseases of the heart and kidneys.

- Exercising is also part of healthy eating as exercise can increase appetite and cause hunger, which improves the individual's food intake.
- They should enjoy a variety of foods and ensure adequate protein intake for maintaining one's muscle mass. A daily protein intake of 1 gram per kilogram of body weight is needed for the elderly.
- A dietary supplement (vitamins, minerals) in the form of a tablet may be taken after consulting with the doctor.

Some suggestions for eating healthy are as follows

- The elderly get tired of eating alone, especially if they are living independently. They can share food with a friend or resort to combined cooking which helps to avoid the monotony of cooking and eating alone. Alternatively, joining a community eating center or religious facility where food is provided should be an option. In the family, the elderly should always be included at the table during the family meals.
- If the person has any dental problems, they should be treated with the help of a dental surgeon.
- The elderly may be encouraged to eat 5 times a day instead of the 3 meals which

they might have been accustomed to. This ensures that the nutritional intake is adequate. Two of these can be healthy snacks with a drink of coffee, tea, or any fruit or vegetable juice.

- For those who have difficulty in chewing due to muscular weakness or dental problems, the food may be given in the form of soups, stews or porridge with added chopped meat or vegetables. Alternatively, smoothies or shakes may be given. Foods like fruits or vegetables may be chopped into small eatable chunks for ease of feeding.

- Spices and herbs may be used for seasoning instead of salt and sugar.

- Snacks may be given in the form of steamed fruits, soft ripe fruits, yoghurt, or low-fat milk. Ripe fruits should be preferred to semi-ripe ones as the former are easily chewable.

- Adequate intake of fiber is needed to prevent constipation. FDA data indicate that about 90% of Americans do not take the daily needed amount of fiber. A daily intake of 25 to 35 grams of fiber is needed in a normal adult. This can be in the form of natural foods rich in fiber like split peas, lentils, black beans, lima beans, artichokes, and raspberries. Nuts, seeds, and all vegetables contain adequate natural fiber. They can also be given in the form of fiber supplements like psyllium, wheat dextrin and methyl cellulose.

Obesity

Obesity has increased over the past two decades globally and in the United States. Obesity increases one's risk of premature death, diabetes, heart disease, stroke, osteoarthritis, and certain types of cancers.

Decrease in physical activity combined with slower metabolism, normal or increased intake of calories and decrease in thyroid function may lead to obesity in an elderly individual.

Serving food in small quantities, consuming foods low in calories and increasing the daily physical activity are some of the methods to counteract obesity.

Food and Medication

Most of the elderly patients may have co-existing diseases and need to take medications. Some of them may have more than five medications per day depending on their illness. Let us briefly see what effect medications can have on the individual's feeding and how food can affect the medications.

- Some medications can upset the stomach and render the absorption of food poor.
- Nausea and vomiting may occur as side effects of some medications. Hence these

medications should be changed to a substitute by requesting the doctor.

- Dizziness, sleepiness, or confusion may be side effects of some medications, and this can seriously affect the individual's eating habits.

- On the other hand, foods also can affect medications. Food can delay or increase the absorption of some medications. It is always important to ask the physician as to the foods which need to be avoided while taking some medications.

- The timing of the medication in relation to the food, before, during or after, should also be clarified.

- Some medications are better absorbed on an empty stomach and others are to be taken with meals or after meals. The patient should get specific instructions from his doctor regarding these.

Some practical tips on feeding the elderly.

Some elderly individuals may become adamant in their needs, and it may be difficult to feed them or coax them to eat food normally. They may behave like children. The caregiver or the relative looking after them should know how to deal with this.

- The meals and snacks of the individual should be made 'Nutrient Dense'. Nutrient dense foods are those that contain plenty of nutrients, but fewer calories. This can be done by meal enrichment. Adding grated cheese, skimmed milk powder to foods like shakes and smoothies increases their nutrient value. Protein powder can be added to porridge to increase the nutrient value.

- A variety of fruits and vegetables should be served.
- Herbs and spices may be used for flavouring instead of using salt and sugar.
- Meals may be made attractive and colorful so that it appeals to the person.
- If the person has chewing problems, the foods may be offered in a semi-solid form like porridge or soups with grated vegetables. Vegetables may be cooked well so that chewing them is minimised and easy.
- Smaller meals and snacks should be served to them instead of three large meals a day.
- They should be dissuaded from consuming non nutritious items like soft drinks, coffee, tea, sodas. Instead, nutritious drinks should be provided.
- The mealtime should be made enjoyable and socially satisfying. In a family, meals may be eaten with the elderly at the table. They should not be served separately and when they are alone.

- Use nutrient supplements whenever needed according to the advice of the doctor. It can be in the form of tablets or powders added to the foods.
- In some societies, services may be available for the elderly like community dining areas, meals delivered at home, home visits by dieticians, and 'Meals on Wheels'. These services should be availed of whenever possible.

DEHYDRATION

Dehydration is a condition where the body loses water which is essential for normal functioning of the body. It is a dangerous condition and is more deleterious in old age compared to the young. It can happen rapidly and can often mislead the caregiver regarding the problem which the person has.

Dehydration can occur either due to poor intake of water and other liquids or due to excess loss of fluids from the body as in vomiting or diarrhea. Mild and moderate dehydration can often be managed at home, but severe dehydration calls for urgent hospitalization and replacement of the lost fluid intravenously.

What are the conditions that can lead to Dehydration.

- o Inadequate intake of water or other fluids is a common cause. The thirst sensation may be reduced in old age and hence an elderly individual may not feel the urge to drink water. This can lead to dehydration.
- o Diarrhea and vomiting due to any cause could lead to dehydration if the fluid lost is not replaced quickly.
- o Certain medicines given for heart and kidney diseases may cause excess urination and lead to dehydration. There are some diseases like diabetes mellitus in which the patient has excess urination and this could lead to dehydration.
- o Fever causes dehydration due to excess loss of fluid from the body.
- o Excess sweating as can occur during exposure to hot climates can lead to dehydration. In hot and dry climates, there may not be sweating and the person may drift into dehydration unknowingly.

How do you recognize dehydration

- o Feeling of excess thirst is the usual symptom in dehydration.
- o The mouth and tongue are dry. Swallowing may become difficult. Saliva production in the mouth is reduced.
- o Excess fatigue is often a sign of dehydration.

- The skin is dry. The 'Pinch Test' can be used to determine dehydration. Pinch a bit of skin in the arm, back of the palm or abdomen. Normally the skin returns to its flat position as soon as it is released. In dehydration, it remains like a ridge for a few seconds taking more time to return to normal. This is because of the loss of skin turgor with dehydration.
- The frequency of passing urine is decreased and the urine is high colored and may have a bad smell.
- They eyes may be sunken in severe dehydration.
- The person may feel dizzy and confused. The person may feel irritable. The blood pressure decreases due to the decrease in blood volume as a result of dehydration.
- Tears in the eyes are reduced. The eyes become dry and itchy.

How can we treat dehydration

Mild and moderate dehydration can be managed at home by replacing the lost fluid orally. Adequate water should be given to drink. Often electrolytes like salt have to be replaced. If the patient is having vomiting, the help of a doctor should be sought. Medications to prevent and control vomiting may be needed. In severe dehydration, the person should be hospitalized and fluids given intravenously.

Oral Rehydration Solution (**ORS**) is a simple solution given to the patient to drink to replace fluids in dehydrated states. It is used especially in children who have diarrhea or vomiting. ORS solution is commercially available and can be dissolved in boiled and cooled water and given to the patient.

At home. ORS can be prepared easily as follows:

To one liter of boiled and cooled water (5 cups of 200 ml each) add half a level teaspoon of salt and six level teaspoons of sugar. Mix well to dissolve the salt and the sugar. This can be given to the dehydrated individual in small quantities frequently till the dehydration is corrected.

How can Dehydration be prevented

1. The elderly individuals should be encouraged to drink fluids including water even if they do not feel thirsty as the thirst sensation may be impaired in them.
2. At least 8 cups of fluid should be taken every day. More fluids will be needed if the ambient temperature is high or if the patient has a fever.

3. At night, the person should ensure that water is available within easy reach on the bedside table so that he does not have to walk to get the water. Warm water should preferably made available in a flask.

4. They should be encouraged to eat succulent fruits and vegetables which provide enough minerals and electrolytes. They should never skip meals.

5. After going out in hot weather, they should routinely drink two or three cups of water to avoid dehydration. Simple drinks prepared from *curd* or *buttermilk* and water with a pinch of salt is an ideal drink in the hot tropic climates. It is called *Sambharam* in South India. Often it is flavored with curry leaves or coriander leaves (cilantro) and a dash of lime and makes an ideal drink in summer.

6. Limit the use of alcohol, coffee, and caffeinated drinks.

7. Ensure adequate intake of water both before and after exercising,

8. The elderly should make it a habit of drinking water at frequent intervals. Reminders may be set in their phone or timers to encourage them to drink more water.

OBESITY

Overweight and Obesity are defined as abnormal or excessive fat accumulation that presents a risk to health. (WHO). A Body Mass Index (BMI) over 25 is considered Overweight and over 30 is considered Obesity. (Refer the section on *Diabetes mellitus*).

It is predicted that by 2030, 20% of individuals in the United States will be over the age of 65. National Health and Nutrition Examination Surveys have shown that the obesity rates in those above the age of 60 is 37.5 % in men and 39.4 in women.

What are the causes of Obesity in old age.

Obesity occurs when a person consumes more calories in the form of food than he spends as energy. This causes accumulation of the excess calories in the body as fat leading to overweight and obesity. Some of the reasons for this increase in weight in old age are as follows.

- After the age of 50, the body needs less calories for its functioning. But if the person continues to eat the same amount of calories he was consuming before, it tends to accumulate as fat in the body.

- Some hormonal changes that occur with aging lead to increased accumulation of fat in the body.
- Genetic factors are also at play. Obesity tends to run in some families.
- Environmental and Sociological factors also contribute to obesity. Lifestyle of certain people and families, the intake of high calorie and unhealthy foods, junk food intake, lack of physical activity due to lack of facilities for exercise, high-calorie, high-fat food available in vending machines especially in the workplace, and non-availability of recreation areas are all implicated in the causation of obesity.
- Poverty and a low level of education have been cited as a causes for increasing weight and obesity. This is more so as packaged foods with high calorie content are cheaper than healthy foods like vegetables and fruits.
- Obesity may be caused by various disease conditions like diabetes, hypothyroidism, polycystic ovary syndrome, and depression.

What are the results of Obesity in the Elderly individuals

Obesity can lead to medical problems which may be life threatening in some individuals and non-fatal in others. Some of the consequences of obesity are:

- Coronary artery disease is often related to obesity and can be life threatening in most of the elderly patients. Often it is the cause of death in them. (See section on *Heart and Circulatory System*).
- Obesity plays an important part in the causation of Diabetes in addition to other factors.
- Obesity is a risk factor for developing gall stones and gall bladder disease.
- Cancers of the breast, kidney, large intestines, and esophagus have been linked to obesity.
- Skin conditions like itching, fungal infections in the folds of the skin like armpit, groin and below the breasts are some of the common problems in obese patients. Obesity also increases the chances of pressure sores if the individual is bed bound.
- Diseases of the bone and joints like Osteoarthritis are more common in the obese, especially in the weight bearing joints like the hip and the knee.
- Respiratory problems like breathlessness due to poor expansion of the lungs is common in obese individuals. Sleep Apnea Syndrome is another common disease in obesity.
- It has recently been reported in studies that obesity is associated with an increase in risk for developing dementia.

How to control weight in the elderly individual

A good environment and social milieu along with a healthy diet can control obesity to a large extent. The control of obesity should start early in adulthood as the person turns 50. Proper diet and exercise are the two pillars on which weight management rest. Some points worth noting are.

- Intake of total fats and sugars should be reduced as age advances.
- Consumption of fruits and vegetables should be increased in addition to lentils, legumes, and nuts.
- Regular physical activity is needs according to one's preference and physical ability.
- Avoiding processed foods which contain high content of fat and sugar.
- Limiting time for watching television or sitting for long periods and avoiding sedentary habits.
- Reducing stress and improving sleep also contribute to reducing obesity.

If the obesity is excessive and cannot be controlled by the above measures, the help of the physician should be sought to try medications to reduce weight and treat any diseases which may be causing the obesity. In extreme cases, the patient may need *Bariatric surgery* to reduce the size of the stomach and thereby reduce absorption of food leading to control of weight.

Resources

1. ESPEN Guidelines on Clinical Nutrition and Hydration in Geriatrics. Volkert D et al. Clinical Nutrition 2019, 38 pages 10-47.
2. Dietary Guidelines for Americans 2020-2025. US Department of Agriculture.
3. Your Golden years. Nutrition for the Elderly.
4. Healthy Eating for Seniors.
5. Nutrition for Older Adults. Medline Plus. National Library of Medicine.

What to know about Dehydration in older adults. Web MD

6. How can I prevent dehydration. Web MD
7. Dehydration. Medline Plus. National Library of Medicine.
8. Addressing Obesity in Aging patients. Batsis JA, Zagaria AB. Medical Clinics of North America. 2018 Jan. 102: 65-85.
9. Obesity in Older Adults. Newman AM. American Nurses Association Periodicals. Vol 14. 2009.

* * * * * *

GLOSSARY

Abdomen The part of the body below the chest containing the organs of the Digestive system, Kidneys, Liver etc.

Acanthosis Nigricans Dark, thick velvety skin in body folds and creases seen in diseases like Diabetes.

Acidosis A condition where there is too much acid in body fluids

Acute Of sudden onset. Sharp.

Aerobic exercise Aerobic means 'related to oxygen'. Exercises which improve cardiovascular fitness

Amino acid An organic compound containing a carboxyl and amino group. They are building blocks from which proteins are formed

Amputation Surgical removal, or cutting off a limb

Anatomy The branch of science dealing with the bodily

281

structure of human and animals.

Anemia Deficiency of red blood cells or hemoglobin in blood

Aneurysm A weakening of the wall of the artery causing an excessive localized enlargement or ballooning

Angina pectoris Chest pain caused by reduced blood flow to the heart

Anticoagulant Medicines that prevents clotting of blood and the formation of blood clots inside the body

Apathetic hyperthyroidism
Hyperthyroidism or excess thyroid hormones causing symptoms like apathy and lethargy, not normally seen in the condition

Arrhythmia A condition where the rhythm of the heart is irregular or abnormal

Arthritis Painful inflammation and stiffness of the joint associated with redness, swelling and reduced mobility

Asbestosis A serious lung condition causing scarring and inflammation of the

	lung caused by asbestos fibers.
Atherosclerosis	A disease of arteries where plaques of fatty material is deposited on their inner walls
Atrophy	Decrease in size or wasting away of a body part or tissue due to degeneration of cells. E.g., Muscle atrophy
Audiometry	A test for measuring the range and sensitivity of a person's sense of hearing
Autoimmune disease	A condition where the body's natural defense system cannot differentiate its own cells from foreign cells (like bacteria) and attacks the normal cells
Autoimmunity	The immune response of the body against its own normal cells causing Autoimmune disease (see above)
Bariatric surgery	Surgery on the Stomach and intestines to help weight loss
Bell's palsy	Paralysis of one side of the muscles of the face due to damage to the Facial Nerve

Benign Paroxysmal Positional Vertigo   A feeling of spinning in the head caused by disturbance in the inner ear

Beta blockers   Medicines used to control Heart Rhythm, Blood pressure and Angina Pectoris

Blood pressure   The force of blood pushing against the walls of the arteries

Body Mass Index (BMI)   Weight to Height ratio calculated by dividing the weight in kilograms by the height in meters squared.

Botulinum toxin   A toxin produced by the Tetanus bacteria. It is a neurotoxin which as injection in small doses is used for medical purposes.

Brain attack   Stroke. Occurs due to sudden blocking of blood supply to part of the brain

Bullae   A large vesicle or blister usually filled with a clear fluid (Singular: **Bulla**)

Butter milk   The slightly sour liquid left after butter has been churned and removed from curd. Used as a drink.

Capillary	Minute tubular blood vessels which are hair like connecting tiny arteries to veins
Carcinogenic	Having the potential to cause cancer ; Cancer inducing
Cardiomyopathy	Chronic disease of the heart muscle
Carpel tunnel syndrome	Painful condition of hands and fingers caused by compression of the nerve in the wrist
Cartilage	Strong, flexible connective tissue that protects the joints and bones acting as a 'shock absorber' in the joints
Cataract	Clouding of the lens of the eye
CDC	Centers for Disease Control and Prevention
Cerebrovascular accident	Medical term for 'Stroke'
Cervical	Relating to the neck or Cervix of the uterus
Chemotherapy	Treatment of Cancer with medications which destroy the cancer cells

Chronic	Long lasting : Persisting for a long time or occurring recurrently (of an illness)
Circadian rhythm	Our physical, mental, and behavioral changes which follow a 24 hour cycle
Cochlea	A hollow tube in the inner ear coiled spirally like a snail shell containing the sensory organ of hearing
Cognition	The mental action or process of acquiring knowledge and understanding through thought, experience, and the senses.
Cognitive decline	A reduction in one or more cognitive abilities like memory, awareness, judgement, and mental acuity
Cognitive function	Multiple mental abilities like learning, thinking, reasoning, remembering, problem solving, decision making etc.
Cognitive Impairment	Same meaning as 'Cognitive Decline'
Co-morbidity	Simultaneous presence of two or

more medical
conditions in a patient

Conjee   A broth or porridge
                      made from rice

Curd   Thick white substance
                      formed when milk
                      turns sour. Used to
                      make cheese

Dehydration   A harmful reduction in
                      the amount of water in
                      the body

Dementia   A chronic disorder of
                      the mental processes
                      due to brain disease or
                      injury leading to
                      memory loss,
                      personality changes
                      and impaired
                      reasoning

Diabetic foot   A foot affected by
                      ulceration in a diabetic
                      often caused by
                      damage to the nerves
                      to the foot or arteries
                      to the lower limb

Diabetic retinopathy A complication of
                      diabetes where the
                      back of the eye (retina)
                      is damaged

Dura mater   A tough outer
                      membrane covering
                      the brain and spinal
                      cord

Dysfunction   An impairment or
                      abnormality in the
                      function of an organ or
                      system in the body

Dysphagia	Difficulty to swallow
Electrolyte	Substances with a natural positive or negative charge when dissolved in water (ions) : In the body they are present in the fluids in the cells, blood, and all tissue fluids. E.g., Sodium, Potassium, Calcium
Epiglottis	A flap of cartilage at the root of the tongue which covers the opening of the windpipe when a person swallows
Esophagus	The part of the alimentary canal that connects the throat to the stomach : The gullet
Estrogen	Hormones which maintain female characteristics of the body. Female Hormones
Fecal incontinence	Inability to control bowel movements leading to unexpected leaking of fecal content (stool) from the rectum
Frailty	The condition of being weak and delicate

Gangrene	Localized death and decomposition of body tissue, resulting from either obstructed circulation or bacterial infection.
Gastroesophageal reflux	A condition in which the acidic fluid in the stomach flows back into the esophagus (food pipe) causing heartburn.
Geriatrician	An expert in the branch of medicine or social sciences dealing with the health and care of elderly people
Geriatrics	The branch of medicine or social sciences dealing with the health and care of old people
Gerontology	The scientific study of Old age, the process of aging and the problems of the elderly people
Gestational diabetes	Diabetes diagnosed for the first time during pregnancy (gestation)
Ghee	Clarified butter used in cooking especially in India. Also used in the religious rituals of Hindus
Glaucoma	A serious condition causing increased pressure within the

eyeball with pain, headache, and gradual loss of vision

Glucagon A hormone produced in the pancreas which promotes the breakdown of glycogen into glucose in the liver thus increasing the blood sugar level. Used to treat low blood sugar levels (hypoglycemia)

Glycated hemoglobin (HbA1c) It is a substance formed in blood by the reaction of glucose with hemoglobin present in the blood. This is measured to know the level of blood sugar control of a patient with diabetes

Goiter An enlargement of the thyroid gland seen in front of the neck

HDL High Density Lipoprotein which is the "Good Cholesterol". It carries cholesterol in blood to the liver to be removed from the body

Hemiplegia Paralysis of one side of the body

Hemoglobin A red protein which carries oxygen in

	blood to various parts of the body. It is present in the red blood cells
Hyperglycemia	Hyperglycemia is the medical term for increase in blood sugar levels above the standard range
Hypertension	Hypertension is the medical term for increase in blood pressure
Hypoglycemia	Hypoglycemia is the medical term where the blood sugar (glucose)level is lower than the standard range
Hypothyroidism	It is a condition where the thyroid gland produces lesser amounts of hormones (underactive thyroid)
Impulse	A wave of excitation transmitted through tissues especially nerves and muscles leading to physiological activity
Inflammation	A localized physical condition in which part of the body becomes reddened, swollen, hot, and often painful, especially as a reaction to injury or infection.

Insulin	A hormone produced in the pancreas which controls the level of sugar (glucose) in blood. Lack of insulin causes Diabetes
Insulin resistance	An impaired response of the body to insulin leading to high blood sugar levels and diabetes
Insulin sensitivity	Insulin sensitivity means how responsive the body is to insulin. A high sensitivity indicates that blood glucose is used more effectively by the body
Intervertebral disc	A thin layer of cartilage separating adjacent vertebrae in the spine acting as a 'shock absorber'
Intravenous	Inside the veins : Medications given as injection into the vein
Larynx	The hollow muscular organ between the throat and the windpipe holding the vocal cords that produce voice : Voice Box
LDL	Low **D**ensity **L**ipoprotein or "Bad Cholesterol" which tends to accumulate

	and cause blocks in the arteries
Ligament	A short band of tough, flexible fibrous connective tissue which connects two bones or cartilages or holds together a joint.
Lumbar	Relating to the lower back : Constituting the loins or the area of the vertebrae between the thoracic vertebrae and sacrum
Maida	A finely milled, refined, and bleached wheat flour, used in making many Indian foods like samosa, chakli, porota and bhatoora.
Malnutrition	Malnutrition refers to deficiencies, excesses, or imbalances in a person's intake of energy and/or nutrients. (W.H.O.)
Marrow	The soft fatty substance filling the hollow cavities of bones in which blood cells are produced
Membrane	A thin layer of tissue or a layer of cells acting as a boundary, lining, partition or

covering in an organism

Metabolic acidosis — Metabolic acidosis is present when there is too much acid produced in the body during metabolism causing excess acid in body fluids

Metabolism — The chemical processes that occur within a living organism in order to maintain life.

Morbidity — The condition of suffering from a disease or medical condition.

Mortality — The state of being subject to death : The state or quality of being mortal

Myxedema — Myxedema is a term generally used to denote severe hypothyroidism causing swelling of the skin and underlying tissues due to a waxy substance in the skin

Nebulization — Conversion of a medication into a fine spray or mist to be inhaled : Used in diseases of the lungs

Obesity — The condition of being grossly fat or overweight

Oncologist	A medical practitioner who diagnoses and treats cancer
Ophthalmologist	A medical specialist who treats disorders and diseases of the eye
Optic nerve	The nerve that connects the back of the eye (retina) to the brain to create visual images : The nerve that helps us see things
Ossicles	A very small bone especially the three ones in the middle ear which help transmit sound vibrations to the inner ear
Palliative	Relieving pain without treating the cause of the condition
Palliative Care	Specialized medical care that focuses on providing patients relief from pain and other symptoms of a serious illness, without treating the primary disease. Palliative care teams aim to improve the quality of life for both patients and their families. It relieves symptoms like pain
Palliative treatment	Palliative care is care meant to improve the quality of life of

	patients who have a serious or life-threatening disease, such as cancer. It can be given with or without curative care.
Pancreas	A large 'bitter-gourd' shaped gland behind the stomach which secretes digestive juices into the intestines. It also produces the hormone Insulin
Paronychia	Inflammation of the tissues around the nail of a finger or toe with infection and pus formation
Pelvis	The large bony structure near the base of the spine to which the hind limbs or legs are attached in humans and many other vertebrates : Pelvis also indicates the broadened, funnel shaped top part of the ureter into which the kidney tubules drain.
Periosteum	The dense layer of connective tissue enveloping the bones except at the surfaces of the joints.
Pharynx	The pharynx is a muscular, funnel-

shaped passageway at the back of the tongue. Also called 'throat'. It connects the mouth and nose to the esophagus (leading to the stomach) and larynx (leading to the trachea and then lungs).

Physiology The branch of biology that deals with the normal functions of living organisms and their parts.

Pneumothorax The presence of air or gas in the cavity between the lungs and the chest wall, causing collapse of the lung.

Polyneuropathy Polyneuropathy means that many nerves in different parts of the body are involved or damaged by the disease. E.g., Diabetic polyneuropathy

Pranayama Pranayama is the practice of breath regulation or breath control. It is a main component of yoga, an exercise for physical and mental wellness.

Pre-diabetes Prediabetes is a health condition that often precedes Diabetes, where blood sugar levels are higher than normal, but not high enough yet to be diagnosed as diabetes.

Presbycusis Age-related hearing loss (or presbycusis) is the gradual loss of hearing in both ears .

Presbyphagia Presbyphagia is a characteristic change in the swallowing mechanism of otherwise healthy older adults causing difficulty in swallowing

Presbyphonia Presbyphonia is defined as aging of the voice and the changes that occur in the voice as a person grows old

Prostate gland The prostate gland is located just below the bladder in men and surrounds the top portion of the tube that drains urine from the bladder (urethra)

Pulmonologist A specialist who diagnoses and treats diseases of the lungs and respiratory system

Rehabilitation The action of restoring someone to health or normal life through training and therapy after addiction, or an illness.

Retina   A layer of cells at the back of the eyeball that are sensitive to light and that trigger nerve impulses that pass via the optic nerve to the brain, where a visual image is formed.

Rheumatic nodules   Rheumatic or Rheumatoid nodules are firm lumps that appear under the skin in up to 20% of patients with Rheumatoid Arthritis. They usually occur over exposed joints such as the finger joints and elbows.

Rhinitis   Inflammation of the inner lining of the nose, caused by a virus infection (e.g., the common cold) or by an allergic reaction (e.g., hay fever).

Sacrum   A triangular bone in the lower back formed from fused vertebrae and situated between the two hipbones of the pelvis

Sambharam   *Sambaram* or *Morum Vellam*

is Kerala (South India) style spicy buttermilk which is spiced with curry leaves, green chillies, and ginger.

Semicircular canals They are three tiny, fluid-filled tubes in the inner ear that help us keep our balance.

Sepsis A serious condition resulting from the presence of harmful microorganisms in the blood or other tissues, potentially leading to the malfunctioning of various organs, low blood pressure, and death.

Signs Any objective evidence of disease in a person (Medical meaning) See *Symptoms*

Sleep Apnea Syndrome Sleep apnea syndrome is a potentially serious sleep disorder in which breathing repeatedly stops and starts

Spasticity Spasticity is a condition in which there is an abnormal increase in muscle tone or stiffness of muscle, which might interfere with

	movement, speech, or be associated with discomfort or pain.
Steroid	Organic compounds which are component of many hormones : Steroids also are medications which are used in treatment of some diseases
Stricture	A narrowing in a hollow tubular structure or organ in the body causing impedance to flow of fluids E.g., Stricture of the Urethra
Stroke	A Stroke or Brain Attack is due to blocking of blood supply to part of the brain : The sudden death of brain cells due to lack of oxygen, caused by blockage of blood flow or rupture of an artery to the brain.
Symptoms	Subjective evidence of disease or physical disturbance observed by the patient : What the patient complains of is a *Symptom*. What the doctor finds on clinical examination is a *Sign*

Synovial fluid	It is the thick joint fluid present inside the joint lubricating the surfaces of the bones during movement to reduce friction
Synovial membrane	The thick membrane which lines the inside of the joints and secretes the synovial fluid
Tendons	A flexible but inelastic cord of strong fibrous collagen tissue attaching a muscle to a bone.
Thoracic	Pertaining to the Chest or Thorax
Thrombosis	It is the formation of a blood clot or Thrombus
Thyroid nodule	Solid or fluid-filled lumps that occur within the thyroid gland
Thyroxine	The main hormone produced by the thyroid gland, acting to increase metabolic rate, and so regulating growth and development.
Tinnitus	Ringing or buzzing in the ears

Tissue	A group or layer of cells that perform specific functions e.g., Muscle tissue
Tympanic membrane	It is also called Eardrum and separates the outer ear from the middle ear. It vibrates when sound strikes it and conveys the vibrations to the middle ear and then to the inner ear for hearing to occur
Ureter	The duct by which urine passes from the kidney to the bladder
Urethra	The duct by which urine is conveyed out of the body from the bladder, and which in males also conveys semen.
Urinary incontinence	Accidental leaking of urine is called Urinary Incontinence
Urinary retention	A condition where the bladder does not completely empty each time a person passes urine
Vagina	The muscular tube leading from the external genitals to the cervix of the uterus in women
Vegan	A person who does not eat any food derived

from animals and who typically does not use other animal products.

Vegetarian A person who does not eat meat, and sometimes other animal products, especially for moral, religious, or health reasons.

Vertebra Each of the series of small bones forming the backbone

Vertigo A sensation of whirling and loss of balance, associated particularly with sudden change in the position of the head caused by disease affecting the inner ear or the vestibular nerve : Giddiness.

Voice fatigue Vocal fatigue or Voice fatigue is when the muscles of the larynx tire out and cause a feeling of pain and weakness of voice

Xanthalesma A harmless, yellow growth that appears on or by the corners of your eyelids next to the nose due to cholesterol deposition under the skin

A Humble Request to the Reader

Thank you for buying and reading this book. May I request your indulgence for one more favour.

I hope you enjoyed reading this book and derived benefit from the various topics discussed.

Kindly give your sincere and valuable review of this book in the Amazon site. Your rating and candid review will be a great inspiration and encouragement to me.

I would also request you to check my other two books – *Tell Me a Story, Grandpa* and *Grandpa Tell Me More Stories* which are a compilation of short stories with morals, mainly written with children in mind.

My book '*In Search of a Bridegroom*' is an interesting Autobiographical Fiction which will be of great interest to the reader.

You can contact me at my email address kvsauthor@gmail.com

https://www.linkedin.com/in/sahasranam-dr-k-v-3231a13a/
(Linked In)

https://medium.com/@ramani2911/membership (Medium.com)

https://www.amazon.com/author/sahasranamkalpathy (Amazon Author Central)

Tell Me A Story, Grandpa

This is the first book written by the author in his 'Grandpa Series'.

Grandpa tirelessly regales children with forty stories from all around. Every story carries a moral at the end for the children to ruminate upon. These stories can keep your children engaged and fascinated during their free time.

"There is a good reason for everything that happens", says Grandpa, "Like the story of the ship-wrecked sailor" and the children immediately pounce upon grandpa to tell them the story of the Ship-wrecked Sailor.

"Don't interfere with your dad while he is painting the patio, your advice is not needed," says Grandpa, "Like the King's Sculptor who was advised by too many people".

There are stories which inculcate Benevolence (The Three Good Deeds), Dedication (Akbar and Tansen) Humility (The Humble Millionaire), Devotion to God (God's Grace), and stories Just for Laughs (The Cure, Oh! Doctor)

And many more such stories in the backdrop of everyday occurrence in the families as a prelude which takes you to the height of imagination and morality.

Grandpa, Tell Me More Stories

This is a collection of forty short stories for children. It is a continuation of the previous book where Grandpa regales his granddaughters with more moral-packed stories. The stories are derived from various sources and endeavour to instil values of truth, justice, and honesty in children.

Do you find that your children are bored? Read them these short stories with Morals, Educational and Entertaining. Both Fiction and Mythology stories are presented. Humorous stories and thought-provoking ones keep the children engaged and enthralled. They make ideal bedtime stories for kids.

The book is a must read by every child and should be the part of every school library.

In Search Of A Bridegroom

This is the third book by the author and describes the problems faced by a parent when he begins searching for an appropriate bridegroom for his daughter.

This is the story of every parent in India and the author portrays the woes of a concerned parent in this 'Autobiographical fiction'.

Once a daughter reaches a marriageable age, it is the duty of the parents to find a suitable bridegroom for her. This is the tradition in Hindu culture. Certain sects of Hindus have rigid rules regarding marriage and choice of a bridegroom. The author, himself a Tamil Brahmin, thought-provokingly chronicles the not-so-pleasant experiences encountered while searching for a suitable boy for his daughter.

The events described in this book are true and takes the readers through a real time accounts of the events as they

ABOUT THE AUTHOR

The author is a practicing Cardiologist. In this book he writes about the Problems of the Elderly individuals. This is written in two parts, this being Part 1 of the book. In a simple, non-medical language, he deals with the medical problems facing the elderly population

He has written two previous books of Short Stories with morals, mainly for children named '**Tell Me A Story, Grandpa**' and '**Grandpa, Tell Me More Stories**.' His third book '**In Search of a Bridegroom**' is an Autobiographical fiction based on his personal experiences.

ACKNOWLEDGEMENTS

I wish to acknowledge with thanks the support given to me by my wife Mohana, who has helped me through thick and thin in my literary pursuits.

All my colleagues in the Author community who helped me choose the title and gave constructive feedback for my previous books. My special thanks are due to Prof. R Krishnan who made available the proceedings of the seminar on 'Problems of the Elderly', Dr. Viswanathan and Dr Jayakrishnan C who provided me with references for the topics on ENT problems and Neurology problems respectively.

Above all, I must place on record my sincere thanks to Mr. Som Bathla, my mentor in this author journey and all the affectionate members of the Author-Helping-Author (AHA) community who have always given me constructive suggestions at various stages of my writing and publishing.

My thanks are due to 'revandesigns' for the beautiful cover designed for this book.

Printed in Great Britain
by Amazon